GERARD G

C000260197

Coping with Suicide
A PASTORAL AID

THE COLUMBA PRESS
DUBLIN 1992

First edition, 1992, published by
THE COLUMBA PRESS
93 The Rise, Mount Merrion, Blackrock, Co Dublin, Ireland

Cover designed by Kevin McAleenan
and prepared for press by Bill Bolger
Origination by The Columba Press
Printed by Billings of Worcester

ISBN: 1 85607 046 8

Acknowledgements

The author and publisher gratefully acknowledge the permission of the following to quote from their copyright material: Abingdon Press, Nashville, for *Dictionary of Pastoral Care and Counselling*; Bolton Press, Atlanta, for *My Son, My Son* by Iris Bolton; T & T Clark, Edinburgh, for *Church Dogmatics Vol III* by Karl Barth; Darton, Longman and Todd, London, for quotations from *The Jerusalem Bible*; Goodliffe Neale Ltd, Alcester, for *Christian Ethics* by Henry Peschke; I.C.E.L., Washington DC, for *Pastoral Care of the Sick* and *Order of Christian Funerals*; Macmillan Publishers, London, for *Silent Grief, Living in the Wake of Suicide* by Christopher Lukas and Henry M Seiden; St Paul Publications, Slough, for *Medical Ethics* by Bernard Häring; Veritas Publications, Dublin, for *Suicide: A Permanent Solution?* by Archbishop Dermot Clifford; The Westminster Press, Louisville, for *Sermons on Suicide* and *Perspectives on Suicide*, both edited by James T Clemons.

Contents

PART FOUR
Ongoing grief ministry

Appendices

Preface

To my parents
Kathleen and Edward Green
who in their living and their dying
taught me about him who is
the resurrection and the life, Jesus Christ.

This book was originally prepared as a Comprehensive Community Development Project for the MAACCD Program at Regis College, Denver.

The book was read and scrutinised by a panel of readers and amended in accordance with some of their recommendations. I hereby acknowledge their help and support – Pat McAnuff, John Joe Cunningham, John McAreavey, Charles Byrne, Peter Devlin and in particular Michael Maginn who acted as an advisor right throughout the project. I also acknowledge the help and support of Geraldine McClory who undertook the impossible task of checking for syntax, punctuation and clarity – her advice wasn't always taken! And finally I am indebted to my sister, Angela McVeigh who word-processed the material, while serving coffee – both without charge – I hope!

Introduction

Not many months after ordination, in my first parish I was called to a home where the sudden death of a young mother had taken place. When I arrived the body of the woman had just been taken by ambulance to the local hospital and her husband had been taken by police-car to the local police station. The neighbours told me that they weren't sure if it had been a suicide or a murder – in fact it turned out that the young woman had taken a massive over-dose of tablets and what had seemed to the neighbours like a violent murderous attack was her husband's was his futile attempt to save her by trying to make her vomit the tablets. 'This is life at its rawest,' I thought. That scene, and the events of the following few days, quickly dispelled any 'I have all the answers' enthusiasm. I realised that I was ill-prepared to deal with the multiplicity of issues that this suicide had raised in the immediate family, in the neighbourhood community and in myself.

Over quite a number of years, I have discussed with many priests the subject of ministering to the families of those who have committed suicide. Usually these discussions took place in relation to particular incidents of suicide and in relation to the needs of particular families. The discussions therefore were usually very practical and I certainly found them helpful. But, like most practical pastoral discussions, because the focus of them is rooted in a particular incident or a particular family, it is difficult to plot even the outline of what might become an acceptable common pastoral approach. In fact, I don't think we were ever certain that there was a body of 'pastoral theory' which might address these situations.

The ministry to the bereaved is a shared ministry, involving the wider family circle, neighbours, friends, the local community and the local community services as well as the pastoral minister.

This book is written to address the needs of a minister in the situation simply because he so very often finds himself not only isolated but carrying the major part of the burden of care. To pastoral ministers who read this book I say: 'You do not walk alone in this ministry. Perhaps your very first function is to call on the community to minister with you and I feel certain that the community will respond – slowly at first, but gradually and with tremendous generosity. Other ministers have found that their greatest support has come from those who themselves were grievers in the past – if you know of some of these, invite them to join you in this shared ministry. I trust that this book will be a help and support to your partnership.' To others who read this booklet may I say: 'Though this book is addressed to pastoral ministers, the ministry to the bereaved is a shared ministry. I hope you too will find this a helpful resource and that together we will recognise that he who 'through his cross and resurrection, freed us from sin and death and called us to the glory that has made us a chosen race, a royal priesthood' will strengthen us in our service to all those bereaved as the result of suicide.'

Though the idea for this pastoral aid did in fact come from particular experiences of dealing with suicide and the families of those who completed suicide, I have tried to incorporate many of the thoughts, ideas and insights which I received either through reading or through conversations and structured interviews with both clergy and family members. I acknowledge, with a deep sense of having been gifted and graced, the sharings of the spouses, parents, adult children and brothers and sisters of a number of people who took their own lives. I acknowledge too the openness of my colleagues in the priesthood who have shared with me their experiences of coping with the pastoral implications when one of their parishioners took his or her own life. These priests, Pat McAnuff, Michael Hackett, John Kearney, Charles Byrne, Peter Devlin, Gregory McGivern and Colum Wright, shared their experiences, their approaches, their concerns, their strengths and their feelings of inadequacy in an open and positive way. I hope that this pastoral aid will help address their needs and the needs of all those who are called to minister to those bereaved by the tragedy of suicide.

Some word of explanation is necessary. Throughout the

book I use the words 'suicide survivor' or 'survivor' to refer to a family-member or friend left behind. This is common usage. The word 'survivor' is not usually used to indicate those who have attempted to take their own lives and who have been rescued or have survived the attempt.

More often than not, I use the male pronoun 'he' or 'him' when referring to those who have committed suicide; it is difficult not to be sexist and it is confusing to use the inclusive 'him/her'. To those who are sensitive I apologise and offer, by way of excuse, the fact that indeed almost all of those who committed suicide in the experience of those who shared with me were in fact male.

On the subject-matter of this pastoral aid, I chose not to include any guidelines for helping, supporting or pastorally ministering to those who were threatening to commit suicide or to those who had attempted suicide, or to the families of either. That entire area of prevention and intervention is a large subject, requiring for itself, I am sure, an entire book. What I have chosen to deal with is postvention, pastoral ministry to the bereaved and grieving family and friends of someone who has committed suicide. In Part One I offer a definition of suicide with some general facts about suicide and a brief synopsis of the Church's teaching on suicide. This is followed by a section entitled 'Community Perception of Suicide' which includes treatment of suicide theory, leading to a pastoral understanding with some brief notes on the epidemiology (occurrence in relation to methods available) of suicide and copycat suicides. In Part Two I deal with immediate support for the grieving family. Part Three covers the subject of preparing and conducting a funeral liturgy of someone who has committed suicide. And in Part Four, I address the ongoing ministry to the grieving family followed by two special sections: 'Helping children to grieve' and 'Supporting young people following a suicide'. The appendices contain a selected bibliography, a template for noting funeral arrangements, some information on the Samaritans and some other material which perhaps might form the beginning of a pastoral minister's own personal collection of helpful and relevant material.

PART I

Suicide:
the facts, the teaching, the theory

The facts

A definition

Suicide can be defined as the act of killing oneself intentionally. Those who have had experience in dealing with suicides (either with those who have committed suicide, in terms of their funerals, or with those who are left behind with their terrible grief and guilt feelings) know that there is nothing simple about suicide. No definition could possibly hope to cope with and adequately describe the multi-faceted phenomenon of suicide, but I think it is important to make a start at a definition so that it might provide some kind of anchor point for discussion. Suicide is the deliberate human act of self-inflicted, self-intentioned death. Some forms of suicide are direct, such as shooting oneself while other forms may be indirect, such as refusing to take actions necessary for self-preservation.

International convention provides for the recording of suicide under one of the following headings:

(1) suicide and self-inflicted poisoning by solid or liquid substances;

(2) suicide and self-inflicted poisoning by gases in domestic use;

(3) suicide and self-inflicted poisoning by other gases and vapours;

(4) suicide and self-inflicted injury by hanging, strangulation and suffocation;

(5) suicide and self-inflicted injury by submersion (drowning);

(6) suicide and self-inflicted injury by firearms and explosives;

(7) suicide and self-inflicted injury by cutting and piercing instruments;

(8) suicide and self-inflicted injury by jumping from a high place;

(9) suicide and self-inflicted injury by other and unspecified means;

(10) late effects of self-inflicted injury.

Records also indicate the age group and sex of those committing suicide. Much of the debate relating to the recording of suicides has centred on the misclassification (often intentional) of the cause of death due to various social factors as well as the understandable reluctance to accord the status (or stigma) of suicide to a death where there is even the remotest possibility of some other explanation. It is generally accepted that among the very many 'open verdicts' at least some of the deaths may well have been suicides.

However, despite the shortcomings of the official records, they do give a clear indication of the trends of suicide both in relation to method and the category of person most at risk.

Epidemiology of Suicide

Incidence and prevalence

Sex: Men commit suicide more than three times as often as women. However women are four times more likely to attempt suicide than are men.

Age: Suicide has been recorded as a cause of death in pre-teen children but this was unusual and for a long time the peak age for suicide was in the 45-55 age bracket. This trend has begun to change in the last ten years and the suicide rate among younger people is rapidly rising and this is particularly obvious in the male 15-34 year old age-bracket.

Methods: Epidemiological studies show a relationship between the availability of necessary materials and the number of suicides due to a particular method; this is particularly well demonstrated in the United States where it has been demonstrated that the number of suicides due to gun-shot wounds is directly related to the number of hand-guns held in each State. This perhaps suggests that at least some suicides are impulsive and that some of these may well have been avoided if the methods were not readily available. Perhaps a corollary to this might warrant mention: Curran,

Finlay and McGarry, in their report, 'Suicide in N. Ireland 1960-86'[1] report an increase in the number of police suicides in Northern Ireland:

> In the decade up to 1973 there were only three police suicides but from 1978 – October 1987 there have been 33. All of these were male ... Thirty-one of the thirty-three RUC suicides since 1978 have been by firearms.

The higher rate of successful suicide for men is undoubtedly related to the methods which they use. Men generally choose much more violent and lethal methods and, among those who study suicides, there is debate as to whether the choice is made in favour of the more violent or in favour of the most effective.

The Church's teaching

Suicide in the Scriptures

The Bible gives us accounts of six suicides, five of which are in the Old Testament, excluding the story of Jonah (Judg 9:54; Judg 16:28-31; 1 Sam 31:1-6; 2 Sam 17:23; 1 Kings 16:18;19) and the other that of Judas Iscariot in the new Testament (Mt 27:3-5). Each of these suicides is recorded without any moral or value judgment. Abimelech (Judg 9:50-55), having been seriously wounded on the head by a stone thrown by a woman, and obviously realising that it was a mortal wound, immediately asked his armour bearer to 'draw your sword and kill me that no one may say of me, "a woman killed him."' The armour bearer readily consented and killed Abimelech. Though the next verse does indeed impute Abimelech, it is not because of his suicide; it is rather because of what 'he had done to his father by murdering his seventy brothers.' Samson (Judg 16:23-31), his two eyes having been put out, and as a prisoner mocked and ridiculed by the Philistines, pulled a building down round them and himself while at the same time praying to God, 'May I die with the Philistines.' Again no judgement is made of Samson's suicidal act and he is later spoken of in the New Testament as one of the 'heroes of faith' and 'who did what is right and earned the promises'(Heb 11:38,33). Saul, wounded in battle, like Abimelech had done before him, asked his armour bearer to kill him, but on this occasion the armour bearer refused and so 'Saul took his own sword and fell on it.' Again no judgement is made of this action or of Saul because of this action. Ahitophel, (2 Sam 17:1-23), disappointed that his military advice to Absalom was rejected in favour of someone else's, 'went home to his own town. Then having set his house in order, he strangled himself and so died.' Zimri (1 Kings 16:8-20), having taken power in Israel by murder and about to be deposed, 'went into the keep of the royal palace, burned the palace over his own head and died.' Finally, the suicide of Judas is recorded in Matthew's Gospel (Mt 27:5): 'And flinging down the silver pieces in the sanctuary, he made off and went and hanged himself.' This account is confirmed somewhat in The Acts of the Apostles (Acts 1:16-20): 'As you know, he bought a field with the money he was paid for his crime. He fell headlong and burst open, and all his entrails poured out.' I think it is important to note that nowhere in the bible do we find those who committed suicide condemned for doing so. It is from this heritage, and under great persecution, that the early church developed and approved the phenomenon of self-sacrifice and martyrdom – oblative suicide!

From the Early Church
St Augustine (354-930 A.D.) led the opposition to suicide from within the Church:

> For it is clear that if no one has a private right to kill even a guilty man (and no law allows this), then certainly anyone who kills himself is a murderer, and is more guilty in killing himself the more innocent he is of the charge on which he has condemned himself to death ... It is significant that in the sacred canonical books there can nowhere be found any injunction or permission to commit suicide either to ensure immortality, or to avoid or escape any evil. In fact we must understand it to be forbidden by the law 'You shall not kill' particularly as there is no addition of 'your neighbour' as in the prohibition of false witness ... suicide is monstrous" [2]

Augustine's view is substantiated by various Church Councils (Council of Nimes, 1184, made the condemnation of suicide part of the Canon Law) until the time of St Thomas Aquinas (1225-74) when he reinforced the view that suicide was sinful.

However, from the fifteenth century, writers both from within and without the Church began to reject the harshness of the Church's condemnation of suicide, a harshness which was in fact expressed in many countries in their civil law and customs. The bodies of those who committed suicide were treated brutally and often too the surviving family and relatives were deprived of their possessions and ostracised. Perhaps the residue of this is in the whispering campaigns of small communities after someone in the locality has committed suicide.

The Church today

The present-day Church's teaching on suicide is contained in the *Declaration on Euthanasia*, published by the Sacred Congregation for the Doctrine of the Faith (*Jura et bona*), 5 May 1980. Article 3 reads:

> Intentionally causing one's own death, or suicide, is therefore equally as wrong as murder; such an action on the part of a person is to be considered as a rejection of God's sovereignty and loving plan. Furthermore, suicide is also often a refusal of love for self, the denial of the natural instinct to live, a flight from the duties of justice and charity owed to one's neighbour, to various communities or to the whole of society – although, as is generally recognised, at times there are psychological factors present that can diminish responsibility or even completely remove it. [3]

The moral question

The moral teaching on the subject of suicide is based on the responsibilities entrusted to a person within the context of the stewardship of his own life. Bernard Häring states:

> Man's bodily life is entrusted to his freedom as its most precious talent. He is not the independent lord of his life but only a steward subject to the sovereignty of God. Christ typifies the extent to which man can dispose of his life: he can even lay it down, if need be, in the service of his fellowman as a witness to faith, hope and love ... Suicide strikingly contradicts the role of man as the faithful steward of his life. If, however, we pronounce such a harsh judgement on suicide, it is because of the decisiveness of such a drastic end, and the word 'suicide' can vary in significance according to the whole context and intent of the person who deprives himself of earthly life ... One who consciously and freely destroys his life is nothing other than a craven deserter who refuses to face the trials of the pilgrim. We must be mindful, however, that in spite of the

17

extreme gravity of the sin of suicide, taken objectively, we may not and cannot judge the subjective guilt of anyone who has wrought self-destruction or attempts to do so.[4]

C. Henry Peschke also considers the subject of suicide and states categorically that it is gravely sinful saying that :

Catholic moral theology rejects every kind of suicide. The reasons are the following:

(a) Man has not the right of ownership over his body and his life. He has only the right of responsible administration and usufruct. The owner and master of his life is God. He gave it to man to use it in the service of the divine plan with man and the world ... Suicide is a violation of God's sovereign rights ...

(b) Suicide is very often, though not always, a crime against a person's dependents and human society. This is the case if someone takes his life without consideration for his responsibilities and obligations towards others ...

(c) Suicide is a violation of one's duty to love oneself and to strive after perfection. The person who kills himself deprives himself of the possibility of any further personal growth. He has refused to bring himself to that full perfection to which he has been called by God.[5]

It is clear then that, while the Church sees suicide as wrong, it is aware of various (and almost universally present) mitigating circumstances. Father Patrick Brennan, Director of Evangelisation for the Chicago Archdiocese, puts it this way:

God has given us life to live in partnership with him, to procreate and help the world. To take one's own life is an act of destruction; so, objectively, it's wrong. We ought to come out and say that more; it's wrong, it's wrong. It's a permanent solution to a temporary problem ... But there has been an evolution in pastoral thought, the emphasis is on compassion and de-moralising. Now we're saying that the person taking his own life, rather than committing a terrible evil, was probably in a pit of hopelessness and acted on various impulses. That mitigates the act in terms of personal moral responsibility. [6]

Archbishop Dermot Clifford, in a Pastoral letter on suicide,[7] asks the question which comes up in most people's minds and spells out the answer:

> One question must come up. Is suicide always seriously sinful? The Church teaches that God, the author of life, is the only one to determine its end. This is his prerogative. No human being has the right to usurp God's authority in this. 'Thou shalt not kill' is God's commandment and it forbids murder on the one hand and suicide on the other. Therefore, if someone with the full use of his reason and free will takes his own life, it is always a grave sin. To assist another to take his own life is equally sinful. A further reason why suicide is wrong, according to the Church's teaching, is that it inflicts damage on the community. Today we see this most clearly in the suffering it causes to families who are left. Rational suicide, therefore, is gravely sinful. However this clear-minded form is rare enough in this country. In our country most suicides seem to be committed by people who are under severe mental stress. Their minds are not functioning rationally and they are not in full control of their actions. The most common description of their state of mind in the books is, 'a sense of hopelessness and helplessness.'

The unpardonable sin?

As in the case of many sudden deaths, but with an acute sense of panic the relatives of someone who has committed suicide often ask, 'Is suicide the 'unpardonable' sin? Has he gone to hell? Is there any chance he got a moment to repent?' Archbishop Clifford has this to say :

> Just as the Lord is the only one who has the authority to call a soul out of this world, he alone is the final judge of the person who has died in this way. He alone knows the heart of each one and the mental state towards the end. He is a God of infinite justice and mercy. We must not usurp his function.[8]

It is difficult to know whether this will ease the particular anxiety felt by the relatives. However there is a temptation in the emotionally charged atmosphere of a family, shortly after receiving the news of (or discovering for themselves) their loved one's suicide, to reassure beyond this – 'No, definitely not, he has gone straight to heaven.' This, I would suggest, is to usurp the function of the 'God of infinite justice and mercy.' Hewett[9] poses this question and answers it as follows:

> Traditional Roman Catholic theology has held suicide to be a mortal sin, partly because it is believed to preclude any possibility for repentance. Protestant theology has offered a necessary correction to this view. As both Barth and Bonhoeffer pointed out, many people die suddenly without having 'repented' of all their sins. To make the last millisecond of a person's life so supremely important is to misunderstand both the worth of our lives and the forgiveness of God. Our lives aren't games of high-stakes poker where one final hand can wipe you out. God judges our lives in their totality. If we accept the premise that God's nature is one of steadfast love and mercy then we must say with Barth: 'If there is forgiveness of sins at all ... there is surely forgiveness for suicide.' (Karl Barth, *Church Dogmatics*, Vol III/4., tr. by A.T. Mackay et al, T. & T. Clark, 1961)

Archbishop Clifford gives us the ready-reckoner quotation from 'Epitaph of a man killed from his horse':

> *Betwixt the stirrup and the ground,*
> *he mercy sought and mercy found.*

Community perception

In studying the community and its various attributes, it is possible to produce many classifications which help to analyse, within that community, various groupings and to compare one grouping to another. Obvious categories suggest themselves: male and female; black and white; Irish and English. When we come to suicide, the classification can be very bluntly 'us and them.' From within the surviving family of a suicide victim, the 'us' is a small number of grieving relatives, charged with emotional explosive power, and the 'them' is everybody outside who is perceived to be watching, judging and blaming 'us'. The surviving family of someone who commits suicide often experience a sense of guilt in relation to the suicide, but undoubtedly a deep sense of shame is the strongest feeling experienced by survivors in relation to the community. The family feel stigmatised by the suicide and under scrutiny from the community. This is particularly so if the members themselves, prior to the suicide, had very negative judgements about suicide. In previous suicides in the community they were part of the 'them' and know well the things that are or can be said; they may well have wondered themselves about those other families and judged suicide to be sinful or a sign of madness or wondered what was wrong in the families where suicide had occurred. Now they are a 'suicide family' themselves, under the microscope of the community, a microscope known in the past to have cruelly aided the dissection of the family. Family bondedness will help the surviving family but that bondedness must be healthy; in many cases it becomes the great psychological game of 'circle the wagons' and keep all 'outsiders' out and the suicide becomes 'our secret – say nothing to anybody about it – it's the family honour at stake here.' Such denial tactics are acutely unhealthy. The pastoral minister, with tact and diplomacy, can break the cycle of the social isolation of the family and he is in that unique position where he can persuade the family to accept community support and persuade the community to support the family.

Theories of suicide
In this section I explore some of the perceptions of suicide which a community may have; some of these perceptions are based on knowledge while many others are inevitably based on ignorance and myth.

There are many theories of suicide and this multiplicity of theories is not surprising when we consider that in many ways every suicide is different from any other. But to establish theory we must look to the similarities. Indeed, as has been said, 'every suicide is different and yet every suicide is the same.' Freud (1856-1939) saw suicide as murder, an act of hostility, the ultimate act of hostility turned inward. This type of hostility in relation to suicide, Karl Menninger (modern-day psychiatrist specialising in suicide theory) categorised under three headings: the wish to kill, the wish to be killed, and the wish to die – the difference being not so much in the act of suicide but in the motivation. Menninger analyses these motives under the characteristics shown by suicides:

> Some suicides exhibit hate, aggression, blame, and a wish for revenge. This set of motives Menninger labels 'the wish to kill.' Other suicides are characterised by guilt, submission, self-blame, and self-accusation. This set of motives, Menninger labels as 'the wish to be killed.' The person wishes to destroy self in order to assuage powerful feelings of guilt. Finally, some suicides exhibit a sense of hopelessness, discouragement, and despair. The person experiencing severe illness or great pain decides that life is not worth living. This set of motives Menninger labels 'the wish to die.'[10]

It is surprising how aware ordinary people are of these three motivational possibilities and their perceptions are often expressed in colloquial comments on suicides: 'He had that much hate in him that he was going to kill somebody sometime – I never thought it would be himself.' 'He blamed himself for what happened the wee girl and he couldn't get over it at all.' 'He just couldn't get his head lifted, everything seemed to be a burden, everything seemed to be going wrong – nobody else thought that, but he did.'

A pastoral understanding

It is impractical to cover all the theories of suicide based either in psychiatry or sociology; what those in ministry are looking for, I would suggest, is a theory leading to a pastoral understanding of suicide, a theory that addresses the concerns of both the 'us' and 'them' communities following a suicide. Faced with a suicide in his community, it is not necessary nor is it possible for the pastoral minister to know in great detail the 'why' of this particular suicide. He can at one time, in the early days of grief, encourage the survivors to ask and continue asking the 'why' of their loved one's suicide and, in the latter days, when grief needs to and can be brought to a closure, encourage the same group to leave that inevitably unanswered 'why' behind them. I believe that it is sufficient to know that the person who has committed suicide experienced in some way a deep-rooted sense of hopelessness and helplessness and, as one writer puts it, haplessness.[11] This 'three H formula,' as it is known, gives us an insight into the minds and indeed perhaps the last moments of life of the suicide victim – adding up to what is described as severe depression. This depression is usually caused by some significant loss or series of losses experienced by the person. Such losses include loss of one's reputation, one's job or one's health or the loss experienced through the ending of a relationship. To the outside observer, the loss may not in fact be real but it has been experienced as real by the suicide victim: 'He thought he was about to lose his job and in his mind he had already lost it.' 'He thought he had cancer; in fact it was an iron deficiency.' The helpless, hopeless and hapless condition has been described by some suicidologists as the 'pressure of unbearable pain.'[12] The suicidal person feels trapped in a corner; believing himself to have exhausted every other solution, which may have included medication, therapy, prayer and many more, he now sees suicide as his only answer. He is not so much wanting to die but sees death as the only solution to escape the 'unbearable pain.' I put this 'pressure of unbearable pain' theory to a number of survivors and, for many, it seemed to describe very adequately their loved one's mental state prior to suicide. For others though, it did not throw much light: 'He had pressure certainly but not that kind of pressure, and certainly he gave no indication of depression.' 'No way! He loved himself far too much. He had no pressure – if he was back here I would tell him what unbearable pain really was.' 'No! He was sick alright but not with unbearable pressure but with unbearable pride.' I believe then that the 'pressure of unbearable pain' theory does indeed illuminate many suicides but not all. Perhaps the expression offered to me by a priest as an all embracing theory is the best: 'At that moment of decision, at that moment of action, the balance of mind was indeed disturbed, and very disturbed.'

The 'Why' of suicide

I return again to the question, 'why' and whereas the question isn't easily answered in individual suicides, I offer here some possible general headings under which the 'why' of suicide can be placed. [13]

(1) *A suicide is committed to escape from an intolerable burden or situation.* Perhaps because of an inability to see or to reason clearly, the suicidal person considers his problems as beyond resolution.

(2) *A suicide is committed to punish the survivors.* There is no more powerful way to punish family or friends than to commit suicide. That desire to punish can be so strong that, as well as stifling the desire to live, it also blocks out any discriminatory factor as to who is punished and how many will suffer.

(3) *A suicide is committed to gain attention.* This is more often said of attempted suicide or it can be said that the successful suicidal act was an attention-gaining device which went too far. In many cases it is difficult to know the precise motivation but what must be recognised is that any person threatening suicide or making a suicide attempt should be taken seriously, for many reasons: some people have attempted suicide just to gain attention and have succeeded; when a person is this desperate to gain attention, he is in serious need of help; and those repeatedly seeking attention through suicide attempts may be inclined to increase the lethality of their efforts, thus increasing the risk of 'success'.

(4) *A suicide may be committed to manipulate others* – threatening suicide or attempting suicide in order to get one's way. Repeated attempts to manipulate in this manner might well elicit the response given in frustration, 'well go ahead and do it.' Here suicide is being used as a weapon, an indication of a real sickness in the person who would attempt to manipulate in this manner.

(5) *A suicide is committed to join a deceased one in death.* Here

the Hindu ritual of *suttee*, whereby a widow sacrificed herself on her husband's funeral pyre, comes to mind, but this ritual is by no means the only demonstration of this motivation. Sylvia Plath, the American poet around whose suicide Al Alvarez based his classic book on suicide, *The Savage God*, committed suicide to rejoin her father who she believed was beckoning her from the grave. In my own experience, one spouse whom I interviewed remembered her husband repeatedly saying of an alcohol and money problem, 'I'll have to talk this over with my mum,' even though his mother had been dead for many years.

(6) *A suicide is committed to avoid punishment.* This perhaps serves to explain the number of suicides inside prisons. The suicidal person, having in some cases already begun to taste the punishment, prefers, because of his confused thinking, death to what the punishment is or is perceived to be. This may not necessarily be the length of a prison sentence or the official prison regime, but may be the prison life as experienced by the person. In a recent case in England, (Inquest January 1991), two prisoners in adjoining cells were found to have hanged themselves. One of them left a note suggesting that he was being sexually abused by other prisoners and that this abuse was being unofficially condoned by some of the prison wardens.

(7) *A suicide is committed as self-punishment.* A person, in his confused state of mind, commits suicide because he believes that for some 'sin' or act which he has done he deserves the punishment of death.

(8) *A suicide is committed to avoid becoming a 'burden.'* The suicidal person sees himself, because of some illness or condition which he has, as a burden to his family or, because of some action which he may have committed or is accused of having committed, being a source of shame or an embarrassment to his family.

(9) *A suicide is committed to avoid the effects of a dreaded disease.* Here the person wishes to spare himself the suffering which he perceives to be associated with the disease; life is soured and death seems imminent anyway. Sometimes even the suspicion of the presence of some dreaded condition is sufficient to precipitate a suicide crisis.

(10) *A suicide is committed to pursue an irrational, impulsive whim.* Here the person dices with death through 'highs' on drugs

or Russian Roulette or extreme forms of 'I dare you'. In this case death is played with and there is an ambivalence toward it.

(11) *A suicide is committed to seek martyrdom.* Nowadays martyrdom is rare though some still choose suicide to make their strongest and, of course, their final political protest.

(12) *A suicide is committed to express love.* The suicidal person is anxious to demonstrate how strong his love really was after a relationship has ended either through break-up, divorce or even death – 'just couldn't live without her' phenomenon.

It must be remembered that any suicide is, and probably most suicides are, caused by a multiplicity of reasons and these may come from a number of the above general categories. One person whom I interviewed in relation to her husband's suicide told me how suicidal she had become and that, at various stages, her suicidal desires stemmed from different reasons; sometimes from the pressure of inner pain which never seemed to lift, other times from her guilt where she felt she had no right to live when he had died, and other times from a wish to go to join her dead husband, to be with him lovingly at times but also to 'really kill him' for what he had put herself and her children through by his choice of violent suicide. This surviving spouse told me that, at her most suicidal moment (she was rescued by one of her children and was able to call the Samaritans), none of the reasons to commit suicide seemed present nor did any of the many reasons she had to live seem pressing. 'At that moment I just didn't care about life or death.'

Myths about suicide

'A little knowledge is a dangerous thing.' This is an expression that is most apt when coming to an understanding of the community's perception of suicide; as has been said before, there are many views about suicide and about the reasons for it. This is inevitable considering that suicide is a problem that has plagued civilisation for countless centuries. What is surprising though is the number of 'myths', some more widespread than others, which surround the subject of suicide; very often they are based on half-truths, particular incidents or sheer speculation. They are dangerous though, because when they 'hinder our knowledge about suicide, they thwart prevention and undermine the crucial support survivors need.'[14] Here are some of the more common myths concerning suicide:

(1) *People who talk about suicide never really do it and those who threaten to commit suicide don't really mean it*. Over eighty per cent of those who commit suicide have given some form of warning beforehand. This warning may be in the form of threats or may be in hints or vague allusions. In whatever form they come, pre-warnings should always be taken seriously.

(2) *Suicide usually happens without warning – just out of the blue.* The no-warning suicide is extremely rare and what appears to be the result of a sudden mind-blowing experience can well be just the ultimate step in a long history of depression – a depression that may well have been camouflaged even by the person leaving the clues to his imminent suicide.

(3) *Those who attempt suicide are fully intent on dying.* Suicide attempts outnumber completed suicides by about ten to one. Professionals who deal with suicide believe that there is a variety of mixed motives, showing very often the ambivalence the suicidal person has towards both life and death – he just wants to get rid of or get away from the awful pain inside himself.

(4) *All real suicides leave a note.* Less than one quarter of those committing suicide leave a note and, of these, often the note is vague and indecipherable. On the other hand, the note may in fact be accusatory and lay blame for the suicide on another person. Edwin Shneidman, the world famous expert on the subject of suicide, has said:

> I believe that the person who commits suicide puts his psychological skeleton in the survivor's closet – he sentences the survivor to deal with many negative feelings, and, more, to become obsessed with thoughts regarding his own actual or possible role in having precipitated the suicidal act or having failed to abort it.[15]

There is certainly no surer way of placing this burden on the shoulders of a survivor than to name him in a suicide note. Shneidman has some comfort for those named or blamed:

> In order to commit suicide one cannot write a meaningful suicide note; conversely, if one could write a meaningful note, one would not have to commit suicide ... Life is like a long letter and the suicide note is merely a postscript to it and cannot, by itself, be expected to carry the burden of substituting for the total document. (Shneidman, *Voices of Death*)

What to do with a suicide note immediately after a suicide, who to share it with, how to interpret it and what credibility-weighting to give to it, are questions that survivors have to face. In time, the disposal of the note can become a problem too, requiring resolution and decision before grief can come to a closure.

(5) *Suicide runs in families.* This particular myth is certainly compounded by statistics which show that a person is nine times more likely to commit suicide if he comes from a family with a prior suicide. But it must be stressed that the reason for this is not a genetic predisposition or biological pre-programming towards self-destruction. There are, however, sociological and biological factors that certainly seem to dispose them towards suicidal behaviour. These can include the genetic predisposition to certain mental diseases that lend themselves (though not inevitably) towards suicide. The sociological factors include the fact that a

prior suicide has created a role-model within a family or it may well trigger a depression about the loved one's suicide, which in its turn leads to suicidal thoughts and tendencies.

(6) *Suicide is a subject you should never mention to a depressed person in case you give him ideas.* This is a belief which causes much anxiety among those who suspect that a loved one may be thinking about suicide. It has also caused a lot of pain to those who suspected but didn't say, and now that their loved one has committed suicide it is too late! If a person is very depressed the thought of suicide will have arisen inside himself and he may well have dismissed it immediately or he may have held onto it and considered it as a real option. By being asked a question like, 'Have you ever thought of committing suicide?' the depressed person is given a chance to air his feelings and the freedom to air them with the full 'gusto' of how they really are. The suicidal person has then been given the opportunity to discuss the issue in the open and has moved at least one step closer to getting the necessary help to finding the right solution to his problems.

(7) *Once a person is suicidal, he is suicidal forever or, conversely, those who try to commit suicide but fail won't ever try it again.* These two quite contradictory viewpoints are held by large sections of the population and neither is universally true. According to many researchers, very few of those who attempt suicide actually want to die. They may be attention-seeking or they are ambivalent towards death and don't realise the full import of their actions. If their suicide attempt is unsuccessful and they receive the proper psychiatric care, then they can move on from this temporary crisis. Nine out of ten people who attempt suicide never try again. However, this is only one side of the coin. The other important statistic is that four out of every five completed suicides have made previous attempts on at least one other occasion. A person whose suicide attempt has failed may, even after treatment and counselling, be still suicidal and, if this is the case, then the previous attempt has not only created experience to ensure success the next time, but also has removed a big psychological barrier to suicide. The chances are the next attempt will be successful. Each individual case of attempted suicide merits its own judgement.

Copycat suicides

Copycat suicides or cluster suicides or suicides by contagion refer to suicides that are grouped together closely in time and in space. In January 1991, *The Irish Times*, in an article by John Waters, reported the following:

> Between April and August 1990, eight young Waterford men were drowned in the same stretch of the River Suir in the city. In the past month, another body was pulled from the river. All of the victims were in their late teens/early twenties; all the drownings happened in the early hours of the morning, at weekends. Not surprisingly, rumour has been rife in the city, with everything from drug-rings to demonic possession being mentioned as possible explanations ... Dr Richard Horgan will be conducting his own study into the deaths. He believes the suicides were an example of the contagion/copycat syndrome, but says this is impossible to prove.

It would seem fairly natural to suppose that, where suicides are clustered in time and space, then some element of contagion or copying is taking place. It should be remembered that imitation alone cannot produce suicides; the ingredients of severe depression, great sense of loss etc. (as discussed under *Theories of suicide*) must also be present. Everyone is exposed to suicide either through reports in the media, general conversation or because a person who has committed suicide is known. If people are closely exposed to suicide, either because the suicide person is a member of the same family or is a close friend, then those suffering from depression or some severe loss may well have found a role-model with whom they can identify. The young are particularly vulnerable to this type of contagion. Recognition of this and identification of those most at risk by the pastoral minister will be the first step in an important pastoral outreach.

When a suicide occurs among the young, those most at risk include his friends, his school or workmates, those in the same social network and those with previous suicidal behaviour. Sometimes they will have had insight into the person's problems and/or intentions to commit suicide and they will feel guilty; sometimes they will watch and see the grief of parents and adult friends and, in their mistaken reasoning, see the 'adult world' as justly punished for their 'failures' in regard to their friend who committed suicide; sometimes they will be awed that through suicide you can 'stop the whole world' and make people think of you. These ideas, coupled very often with a suspended awareness of both the fact that death is permanent and that the suicide victim himself received no satisfaction from any of the events which happened after his death, create a temptation to become a copycat. The pastoral minister is in a unique position to alert the community to this situation; to present the reality of the permanence of death; to remove the prestige that suicide may have accorded to the victim; to acknowledge the victim as someone who was deeply disturbed and who had not found a way to work through his problems and to invite those who are now feeling troubled or suicidal to seek help.

PART II

Immediate grief support

There are no standard ways in which news of a suicide comes, but when that news does come it requires the immediate activation of all the resources, both spiritual and emotional, of the pastoral minister. Called to the scene, the pastoral minister can be introduced to perhaps the most horrific sight he will have ever experienced and to have to initiate prayer in this situation will demand composure, 'above and beyond the call of duty.' The minister, I think, should remember that he is human and that to experience shock or even revulsion can be very normal; 'I just couldn't believe that I was so affected by the sight. I was in a state of shock myself,' one very experienced priest confided. He continued, 'It isn't a thing you get over in a day or two.' But the challenge will be to 'rise above' this and to minister in the situation. What is the pastoral minister's role in the situation in relation to the deceased and the relatives (the suicide survivors)? Wasena F. Wright, Jr. says:

> Wherever or however suicide occurs, it is tragic. It brings great sadness and confusion into the lives of all those involved in the life that is gone. The Church ought to be there to symbolise the presence of Almighty God to those affected by the tragedy. The Church ought to be there to assure loved ones that there is a loving God who cares and understands – One who was revealed in the person of Jesus Christ, who shared the grief of the family and friends of his friend Lazarus at the news of his death .[16]

In the *General Introduction to the Pastoral Care of the Sick,* Article 15 states:

> When a priest has been called to attend those who are already dead, he should not administer the sacrament of anointing. Instead he should pray for them, asking that God forgive their sins and graciously receive them into the kingdom. But if the priest is doubtful whether the sick person is dead, he may give the sacrament conditionally. [17]

In Chapter Seven, under the heading 'Prayers for the Dead,' Article 224 states:

> It may be necessary to explain to the family of the person who is dead that sacraments are celebrated for the living, not for the dead, and that the dead are effectively helped by the prayers of the living. [18]

Because of the traditional 'stigma' attached to death by suicide, and because of a tradition of anointing even up to a few hours after someone has 'breathed their last,' it might be very important for the minister to ascertain if this had caused any concern and, if so, to assure the relatives of the one who has committed suicide that the manner of death had nothing whatsoever to do with the body not being anointed. The minister will be able to judge the reactions in the situation and make his decision there and then. Article 225 states:

> To comfort those present the minister may conclude these prayers with a simple blessing or with a symbolic gesture, for example, making the sign of the cross on the forehead. A priest or deacon may sprinkle the body with holy water.[19]

A gesture such as this will mean a great deal to the relatives of anyone who has died without the sacrament of anointing, but especially for the relatives of those who have died as a result of suicide.

Familiarity with the *Pastoral Care of the Sick, Rites of Anointing and Viaticum* will help the priest select the most suitable prayers and readings. If the scene of the suicide is the person's home, then it is likely that there will be very close relatives present when the priest arrives. However it is unlikely that anyone else at the scene will be in a position to help in leading the prayers and the priest will usually have to lead all the prayers himself. I think it is important to involve people in prayer from the very beginning of their bereavement, and so prayers with which people are familiar and traditional invocations with traditional responses are recommended. I would suggest that prayers at the scene of the suicide with the body present should be short but not rushed and should perhaps be continued in another place, or another room, after the body has been removed.

This prayer from the *Pastoral Care of the Sick* is particularly suitable:

> Loving and merciful God,
> we entrust our brother/sister to your mercy.
> You loved him/her greatly in this life:
> now that he/she is freed from all its cares,
> give him/her happiness and peace forever.

The old order has passed away:
welcome him/her now into paradise
where there will be no more sorrow,
no more weeping or pain,
but only peace and joy
with Jesus, your Son, and the Holy Spirit
for ever and ever.
Amen.

And this short reading from St Luke's Gospel is also appropriate:

A reading from the Holy Gospel according to Luke.

It was now about the sixth hour and, with the sun eclipsed, a darkness came over the whole land until the ninth hour. The veil of the Temple was torn right down the middle; and when Jesus had cried out in a loud voice, he said, 'Father, into your hands I commit my spirit.' With these words he breathed his last.

This is the Gospel of the Lord.

Breaking the news

What if the pastoral minister is called to break the news of a suicide to the immediate family? There is no easy way to break the news of a sudden death to family members and it is perhaps the most painful duty of all to tell relatives that their loved one has committed suicide. Yet it is a duty which those in ministry should not shirk. I can only offer the following guidelines:

When he hears the news, he should try to get as much information as is possible and note it down accurately; establish the identity of the informant and then of the person who has committed suicide, his name and address; establish the name and address of the next of kin whom he is being asked to inform; ascertain how and when the death occurred and who can be contacted for further information.

I try to check this kind of information by a return phone-call. Cruel, misguided and 'sick' people are not above using the priest to convey false information.

The pastoral minister will want to convey the information he has received as soon as he possibly can and as accurately as he can. It is difficult to know what to say, but experienced ministers strongly argue that they would not shy from saying that it is suspected or it is known that the person took his/her own life. Some relatives have shared how in their pain they deeply appreciated the gentleness of how the news was broken to them – they were told that their relative was dead and then in a few minutes told that the death had been by suicide.

It is good practice to contact the original informant to confirm that the message has been conveyed.

At this time the family will need a circle of support from the wider family circle and from the neighbours. This is not always easy to arrange, as one priest shared: 'This couple had no close relatives and the neighbours had suffered a lot from them because of drink, so it wasn't easy to rally them even in these circumstances.' But people need others to be around them at this time.

In situations of death and bereavement, I like, as soon as possible, to invite all to pray, recalling the mercy and compassion of God.

Presence of the police
The presence of police in the hours and days after a suicide in a family can be very distressing. On the one hand, it is the duty of the police to investigate every sudden death and to satisfy themselves even though it may be obvious to everyone else that the death was by suicide and that no foul play by others was involved. Relatives feel vulnerable, feel under scrutiny and almost accused by the presence of the police. It is a difficult situation for relatives and police and both sides may welcome the presence and the good offices of the minister in the situation. Questions have to be asked and answers given and this can heighten the tension in an already stress-filled situation; the minister's unobtrusive presence at the interviews can ease this tension, curbing perhaps the insensitivity of an overzealous police officer and yet helping them to satisfy themselves as to the true nature of the tragedy.

It would be impossible to cover in this guide every eventuality, but a number of practical issues, to which *caveats* might be offered, spring to mind. These are not necessarily suicide-related but are offered here as having arisen from research into the survivors of suicide.

Into shock

The pastoral minister is not a doctor and would not normally recommend that bereaved people should take tablets or medication. One woman told me that, on hearing the news of her son's suicide, she was immediately prompted by her family to take medication. She had decided that she wanted to face the situation with her full faculties and without the aid of medication, and her own words are telling: 'I was able to resist our own ones giving me tablets and I was glad when Father ... refused to support them on this. I don't think I could have resisted his persuasion and I would have hated him for it. In the end, his confidence in me was the beginning of healing for me.' The priest will realise that, in the aftermath of a suicide, relatives will go into shock. It is the system's natural way of coping. People are normally allowed to go into shock and remain there at least for sometime, undoped, before coming out again to face what for them are 'the cruelties of life'.

Division in the family

Suicides very often split families and there usually begins a process of blaming and scapegoating. The minister will be particularly sensitive to this and, while being a ready listener, he will not take sides in any family dispute that arises but, perhaps with the firmness that only a pastoral minister can exercise in the situation, help each relative to come to terms with his or her own grief.

Children

Grieving children are difficult to deal with – very often they are pushed to the background, farmed out to relatives and sometimes even denied the truth that their parent or their brother or sister is dead. Pastoral ministers find dealing with grieving children particularly difficult – we don't know what they know; we don't know what to say; and we don't know how to say it. Ministers can encourage relatives to tell the truth to children, both that their loved one is dead and, if it is the case, that he or she took his or her own life. In a later section I will consider how best to help children cope with grief, but in the immediate aftermath of grief it is important that they are present with their closest, that they are told the truth and that they are not burdened with heavy responsibilities, like 'You'll look after mummy now,' or 'You're the man of the house now,' or 'You're daddy's only girl left.'

Something to hold on to

Finally in this section on immediate grief support, I recall something I learned in primary school about boats and ships – as soon as something goes wrong, as soon as serious difficulty arises, they either drop anchor or head for port. The pastoral minister can help survivors of suicide find an anchor, something to hold on to in the days and weeks and months and even years ahead. I think he can also head them in the direction of calmer waters. Iris Bolton, in her book, *My Son... My Son...*, tells of how her counsellor offered 'no trite panaceas' of healing after her son, Mitch, had committed suicide; he told herself and her husband of how they might expect to be in emotional shock for a while, giving way to moments of denial, bargaining and guilt, and experiencing too anger and depression. Then he offered them what I consider to be an anchor and a pointer to calmer waters: 'The first thing,' the doctor said, 'is that this crisis can be used to bring your family closer together than ever. If you use this opportunity wisely, you can survive and be a stronger unit than before ... The formula is simple. Make every decision together throughout this crisis. Hear every voice. Work for consensus. Never exclude your children during these next few days. Call family conferences. Discuss each problem openly, treating each individual equally, regardless of age or experience. Today each of you is hurting in his own unique way. You can blame each other and destroy one another. Or you can share and be supportive. Grief of itself is a medicine when you are open about it. Only secret grief is harmful. Through mutual helping, you will all heal more rapidly, and you will all survive. The choice is yours ... The second thing is more difficult to grasp. You have no reason as yet to believe what I am going to tell you, but I ask you to hear me with an understanding heart. There is a gift for you in your son's death. You may not believe it at this bitter moment, but it is authentic and it can be yours if you are willing to search for it. To other eyes it may remain hidden. The gift is real and precious and you can find it if you choose.'[20]

Iris Bolton shares how the first part of the doctor's advice was acceptable and filled with common sense but the second part was both strange and unbelievable. However, because of her trust in this counsellor, she accepted both. In the days of immediate grief, all decisions were family decisions and this certainly helped the family survive together; in the months afterwards, she searched for the gift and found it in the work she was later to do with the survivors of suicide.

In dealing with the survivors of suicide, it is important to tell them at the outset what to expect. An angry surviving spouse of a suicide shared, 'The priest should have told me what to expect, what it might be like. I couldn't understand what was going on inside myself – it wouldn't have frightened me as much if he had told me. It would have made it so much easier if he had been up front with me.' The pastoral minister perhaps could explain to survivors what they will have to go through; allow them to share their initial anger, frustration and loneliness and then offer them an anchor to hold on to and point them in the direction of calmer waters. Encourage them to talk and to share decision-making, encourage them to create times for being together. This will set them on the right road for surviving. As for the idea of finding a gift in the situation, I found difficulty with this idea at first but I put it to a number of survivors and some identified with it quite readily. In our faith tradition we have a simple way of looking at things, that out of every situation, good or bad, God brings out good. In the time immediately after a death by suicide, it is important to encourage families to talk and share decisions and also to know that somewhere, out of all their pain and agony and suffering, God will draw some good. This good will not be immediately apparent and when it comes it may be different for different people or it may be recognisable to some and not to others, but:

> Those who went sowing in tears
> now sing when they reap.
> They went away, went away reaping
> carrying the seed;
> they come back, come back singing,
> carrying their sheaves. (Ps 126:5-6)

PART III

The Funeral Liturgy

'In the face of death, the Church confidently proclaims that God has created each person for eternal life and that Jesus, the Son of God, by his death and resurrection, has broken the chains of sin and death that bound humanity ... The proclamation of Jesus Christ "who was put to death for our sins and raised to life to justify us" (Rom 4:25) is at the centre of the Church's life. The mystery of the Lord's death and resurrection gives power to all of the Church's activity. "For it was from the side of Christ as he slept the sleep of death upon the cross that there came forth the sublime sacrament of the whole Church." The Church's liturgical and sacramental life and proclamation of the Gospel make this mystery present in the life of the faithful ... At the death of a Christian, whose life of faith was begun in the waters of baptism and strengthened at the eucharistic table, the Church intercedes on behalf of the deceased because of its confident belief that death is not the end nor does it break the bonds forged in life. The Church also ministers to the sorrowing and consoles them in the funeral rites with the comforting word of God and the sacrament of the Eucharist ... Christians celebrate the funeral rites to offer worship, praise and thanksgiving to God for the gift of a life which has now been returned to God, the author of life and the hope of the just. The Mass, the memorial of Christ's death and resurrection, is the principal celebration of the Christian funeral ... The Church through its funeral rites commends the dead to God's merciful love and pleads for the forgiveness of their sins. At the the funeral rites, especially at the celebration of the eucharistic sacrifice, the Christian community affirms and expresses the union of the Church on earth with the Church in heaven in the one great communion of saints. Though separated from the living, the dead are still at one with the community of believers on earth and benefit from their prayers and intercession. At the rite of final commendation and farewell, the community acknowledges the reality of the separation and commends the deceased to God ... The celebration of the Christian funeral brings hope and consolation to the living. While proclaiming the Gospel of Jesus Christ and witnessing to Christian hope in the resurrection, the funeral rites also recall to all who take part in them God's mercy and judgement and meet the human need to turn always to God in times of crisis.'[21] (Extract from *Order of Christian Funerals, General Introduction.*)

Funerals are not liturgies for which we have much prior training and/or theological grounding and they are perhaps 'institutions' that we take very much for granted without a great deal of reflection on their purpose and their effect. At the funeral of a person who has committed suicide, the family of mourners and the community in general are usually more keenly sensitive to what happens or doesn't happen and therefore the messages conveyed through the funeral liturgy on this occasion are more liable to influence both the family and the wider community.

Funerals in general
Throughout the different cultures of the world, and in spite of the variety of ways that funeral rites are carried out, there are some striking similarities, suggesting that there are universal needs which exist at the time of death and that these rituals fulfil these needs. The similarities include the following:

- Social support is provided to grievers through the gathering of relatives and friends. There is an extension of sympathy and empathy, recognition of loss, and communication of care and support aimed at bringing comfort and support to the bereaved.

- Some sort of ritual and ceremony is involved. Often, but not exclusively, the ceremony may be religious in nature, utilised to explain the reason for and meaning of death.

- Visual confrontation of the dead body is common. This may occur at the place of death, the home of the deceased, the funeral home, or a neighbourhood meeting place. The body may be prepared in different ways but is generally put on display.

- There usually is a procession. This can be viewed as a 'family parade' that enables individuals to display their grief publicly. It frequently concludes the funeral, ending at the place of final disposition.

- Some kind of sanitary disposition of the body is carried out. This includes burial, entombment, or cremation. In instances of donation of the body to science, embalming or some form of sanitisation of the body occurs.

- Funerals generally require material expenditure. This

43

enables the bereaved to communicate their loss to society and support this sentiment with tangible, measurable means.

• Funerals serve as severance rites to separate the deceased from the living; rites of passage for mourners to psychologically, socially and spiritually assist them through bereavement; and means of providing societal continuity and affirmation, expression of beliefs and values and group solidarity.[22]

Planning the Funeral

When pastoral ministers plan funerals with the bereaved, they must remember the purpose and function of the funeral, paralleling the three tasks of grief work:

- emancipation from the bondage of the deceased;
- readjustment to the new environment in which the deceased is missing;
- formation of new relationships.

In the recent past, the revised Catholic liturgy for funerals has emphasised the theme of resurrection:

In him who rose from the dead, our hope of resurrection dawned, the sadness of death gives way to the bright promise of immortality. Lord, for your faithful people life is changed, not ended. When the body of our earthly dwelling lies in death, we gain an everlasting dwelling place in heaven.' (*Preface of Christian Death 1*).

This hope-filled liturgy has, in many of its adaptations, failed to address the very human needs of mourners. The reality of grief, loss, sadness and mourning, acknowledged in the liturgy, is lost amidst inappropriate alleluias.

It is perhaps wrong to talk about 'getting the flavour right' in relation to funerals, but maybe the expression conveys accurately a serious responsibility of the minister as he faces the awesome task of beginning to plan a funeral liturgy, particularly the funeral liturgy of someone who has committed suicide. Through the liturgy, the minister will want to address the real concerns of the community. He will familiarise himself with the circumstances of the death and the wide spectrum of opinion, and often conflicting attitudes of the community to which the deceased belonged. He will have to take care of his own personal concerns, anxieties and grief; the more intimately acquainted he was with the deceased, or with the family of the deceased, the more his own grief will be heightened. A pastoral minister would be very unwise to ignore or fail to attend to his own thoughts, emotions, feelings and grief at this time. It may be that he will seek out guidance and help from his director or from more experienced colleagues. In any event, he will be deeply aware that the funeral liturgy will call for a real 'collect' of sentiments and prayers and that these cannot and should not be his alone.

The minister planning an appropriate liturgy with the bereaved family will be aware that he needs to spend some time with the family. A quiet time, usually only possible early in the morning, is perhaps the best time. The priest should arrange a time to call at the home so that all those concerned can be present. He should resist the temptation to arrange the funeral liturgy with the oldest male or with 'the one who appears the most sensible.' Many of the women-survivors with whom I spoke found themselves stuck in the grief process because they were not consulted and were therefore totally unaware of what was happening at their loved one's funeral. The funeral liturgy is as much for the living as it is for the dead, and is clearly the opportunity afforded by the believing community for the bereaved to say goodbye. We cannot deny that opportunity to grievers. The minister, aware that 'blood-relationship' does not always indicate closeness, might be in a position to invite comment and input on funeral arrangements from other mourners, outside the immediate family circle.

The usual areas for discussion in planning the funeral liturgy will include the music, the readings, bidding prayers and the homily, as well as the time, the church and the detail of 'who does what?'

The Music
Some pastoral ministers shy away from a discussion of the music and hymns for funerals, trusting that the family will settle for the well-known traditionals such as 'Nearer my God to thee' or 'Abide with me.' The great fear is that the family will say something like, 'His favourite song was, (and then name some well known popular song). He sang it at every party. He would just love it at his funeral.' On a number of occasions, I have had to instruct singers

that they were not to sing well-loved favourites like, 'I'll take you home again Kathleen,' 'Oh Danny Boy,' and 'From a candy store on the corner to the chapel on the hill.' On one occasion an organist defied church guidelines and played, 'A Whiter Shade of Pale' to commemorate how a twenty-six year old cancer victim looked just as he died. Perhaps the best way to introduce a discussion on the music for a funeral is to say, 'Have we any ideas about what sacred music or what hymns might be most suitable?' It may be necessary to say that, because our funeral liturgy is the celebration of Mass, this precludes the playing of songs other than sacred hymns. In cultures where there are other rites such as viewing in the funeral parlour, the opportunity for the playing of 'favourite songs' is available. When someone seems extremely disappointed that their loved one's favourite song is not going to be played, the minister might suggest that it could be played softly in the home of the deceased or in the funeral parlour prior to the body being removed to the church for Mass. In helping people select hymns or sacred music for the funeral Mass, I try to be conscious of the limits as well as of the breadth of the repertoire of the organist and the community, as well as the possibility of getting someone to lead the singing.

The readings

It is difficult for people to select readings at a moment's notice; it is better to leave a selection of readings with the family, perhaps on the night before. The booklet, *Through Death to Life, Preparing to Celebrate the Mass of Christian Burial*, by Joseph Champlin,[23] offers an entire selection of suitable readings from both the Old Testament and the New Testament. It should be made clear to people, preferably by leaving some written guidelines, that they should normally choose a First Reading from the Old Testament, a Responsorial Psalm and a Second Reading from the Epistles. I have included in the appendices a page which might be photocopied and left with the family and could then be completed when they had made their choices. Clergy often like to choose the Gospel reading themselves, particularly since it will be to that text that their homily will most relate; however, to select the Gospel in consultation with the family can mean a lot to them.

Are there some readings unsuitable for the funerals of suicide victims? Having reviewed the readings presented in the Lectionary in the section, *Masses for the Dead*, I would suggest that everyone of them could speak strongly to the bereaved but it could be said that some are more suitable than others. Here I present two from each category which have been suggested to me by priests as being very suitable. (The two sample liturgies will be based on these readings.)

From the Old Testament
Reading 4 : A Reading from the Prophet Isaiah (Is 25:6-9)
(The Lord will destroy death forever.)

On this mountain, the Lord of hosts will prepare for all peoples a banquet of rich food. On this mountain he will remove the mourning veil covering all peoples, and the shroud enwrapping all nations, he will destroy Death for ever. The Lord will wipe away the tears from every cheek; he will take away his people's shame everywhere on earth, for the Lord has said so. That day, it will be said: 'See, this is our God in whom we hoped for salvation; the Lord is the one in whom we hoped. We exult and we rejoice that he has saved us.'

Reading 5 : A Reading from the Book of Lamentations (Lam 3:17-26)
(It is good to wait in silence for the Lord to save.)

My soul is shut out from peace; I have forgotten happiness. And now I say,'My strength is gone, that hope which came from the Lord.' Brooding on my anguish and affliction is gall and wormwood. My spirit ponders it continually and sinks within me. This is what I shall tell my heart, and so recover hope: the favours of the Lord are not all past, his kindnesses are not exhausted; every morning they are renewed; great is his faithfulness. 'My portion is the Lord,' says my soul, 'and so I will hope in him.' The Lord is good to those who trust him, to the soul that searches for him. It is good to wait in silence for the Lord to save.

Responsorial Psalm
Psalm 129
Response: Out of the depths, I cry to you, O Lord.

> 1. Out of the depths I cry to you, O Lord
> Lord, hear my voice!
> O let your ears be attentive to the voice of my pleading.

> 2. If you, O Lord, should mark our guilt,
> Lord who would survive?
> But with you is found forgiveness:
> for this we revere you.

> 3. My soul is waiting for the Lord,
> I count on his word.
> My soul is longing for the Lord
> more than watchman for daybreak.

> 4. Because with the Lord there is mercy
> and fullness of redemption,
> Israel he will redeem from all its iniquity.

Psalm 102: 8,10,13-18
Response: The Lord is compassion and love.

> 1. The Lord is compassion and love,
> slow to anger and rich in mercy.
> He does not treat us according to our sins
> nor repay us according to our faults.

> 2. As a father has compassion on his sons,
> the Lord has pity on those who fear him;
> for he knows of what we are made
> he remembers that we are dust.

> 3. As for man, his days are like grass;
> he flowers like the flower of the field;
> the wind blows and he is gone
> and his place never sees him again.

> 4. But the love of the Lord is everlasting
> upon those who hold him in fear;
> his justice reaches out to children's children
> when they keep his covenant in truth.

Second Readings

Reading 5
A Reading from the letter of St Paul to the Romans (Rom 8:31-35,37-39)
(Nothing can come between us and the love of Christ.)

With God on our side who can be against us? Since God did not spare his own Son, but gave him up to benefit us all, we may be certain, after such a gift, that he will not refuse anything he can give. Could anyone accuse those God has chosen? When God acquits, could anyone condemn? Could Christ Jesus? No! He not only died for us – he rose from the dead, and there at God's right hand he stands and pleads for us.

Nothing therefore can come between us and the love of Christ, even if we are troubled or worried, or being persecuted, or lacking food or clothes, or being threatened or even attacked. These are trials through which we triumph, by the power of him who loved us.

For I am certain of this: neither death nor life, no angel, no prince, nothing that exists, nothing still to come, not any power, or height or depth, nor any created thing, can ever come between us and the love of God made visible in Christ Jesus our Lord.

Reading 14
A Reading from the First letter of St John (Jn 3:1-2)
(We shall see him as he really is.)

Think of the love that the Father has lavished on us, by letting us be called God's children; and that is what we are. Because the world refused to acknowledge him, therefore it does not acknowledge us. My dear people, we are already the children of God but what we are to be in the future has not yet been revealed; all we know is, that when it is revealed we shall be like him because we shall see him as he really is.

Gospel Readings

Reading 5
A reading from the holy Gospel according to Mark (Mk 15:33-39;
16:1-6)
(Jesus gave a loud cry and breathed his last.)

When the sixth hour came there was darkness over the whole land until the ninth hour. And at the ninth hour Jesus cried out in a loud voice, 'Eloi, Eloi, lama sabachthani?' which means, 'My God, my God, why have you deserted me?' When some of those who stood by heard this, they said, 'Listen he is called on Elijah.' Someone ran and soaked a sponge in vinegar and putting it on a reed, gave it to him to drink saying, 'Wait and see if Elijah will come to take him down.' But Jesus gave a loud cry and breathed his last. And the veil of the Temple was torn in two from top to bottom. The centurion, who was standing in front of him, had seen how he had died and he said, 'In truth this man was a son of God.'' When the sabbath was over, Mary of Magdala, Mary the mother of James, and Salome, bought spices with which to go and anoint him. And very early in the morning on the first day of the week they went to the tomb just as the sun was rising. They had been saying to one another, 'Who will roll away the stone for us from the entrance to the tomb?' But when they looked they could see that the stone – which was very big – had already been rolled back. On entering the tomb they saw a young man in a white robe seated on the right-hand side and they were struck with amazement. But he said to them, 'There is no need for alarm. You are looking for Jesus of Nazareth, who was crucified; he has risen, he is not here. See, here is the place where they laid him.'

Reading 17
A reading from the holy Gospel according to John (Jn 14:1-6)
(There are many rooms in my Father's house.)

Jesus said to his disciples : 'Do not let your hearts be troubled. Trust in God still, and trust in me. There are many rooms in my Father's house; if there were not, I should have told you. I am going now to prepare a place for you, and after I have gone and prepared you a place, I shall return to take you with me; so that where I am you may be too. You know the way to the place where I am going.' Thomas said, 'Lord we do not know where you are going, so how can we know the way?' Jesus said: 'I am the Way, the Truth and the Life. No one can come to the Father except through me.'

Preaching the funeral homily

A brief homily based on the readings is always given after the gospel reading at the funeral liturgy and may also be given after the readings at the vigil service; but there is never to be a eulogy. Attentive to the grief of those present, the homilist should dwell on God's compassionate love and on the paschal mystery of the Lord, as proclaimed in the Scripture readings. The homilist should also help the members of the assembly to understand that the mystery of God's love and the mystery of Jesus' victorious death and resurrection were present in the life and death of the deceased and that these mysteries are active in their own lives as well. Through the homily the members of the family and community should receive consolation and strength to face the death of one of their members with a hope nourished by the saving word of God. Lay persons who preside at funeral rites give an instruction on the readings.[24] (*General Introduction, Order of Christian Funerals*, Article 27).

Preparing and preaching the homily for any funeral is a particularly difficult task and when the death is due to suicide then further complications can challenge the spiritual as well as the homiletic resources of any minister. That 'it's not easy' will be a sentiment shared by all who have faced this task and these notes are by way of assistance rather than offering any definitive guidelines on the preparation and preaching of the homily.

How some have approached the homily is perhaps indicated by the following quotations from interviews with clergy:

The whole thought of 'why', I felt, was the question dominating the previous two days. I addressed that and then explained that the manner in which we die bears no relationship to the way God receives us. At death we are given the opportunity to make a final choice for God. The most of (deceased's) life would certainly indicate that he made that choice for God.

I wanted to say this isn't God's plan ... I was at pains not to glorify the death; at the same time I wanted to give comfort and some sort of meaning to the suffering.

Whatever happened was between the deceased and God – it wasn't our place to judge or even to pass comment. I explained too that God is a God of love, a God of mercy and a God of understanding.

I said it was so tragic and that we may never know why and we should not presume to judge.

A proclamation of God's mercy and compassion

The funeral homily is first and foremost a proclamation of the mystery of God's compassion which is demonstrated in the relationship of God with his chosen people, culminating in his sending of his Son, Jesus Christ, who 'chose to die that he might free all men from dying' and in whom 'the hope of resurrection dawned.' However, because in the Catholic Church the funeral liturgy is usually the only public ritual of passage, and the homily the only opportunity of public expression of sympathy, a funeral homily which does not mention the dead person is clearly insensitive. It has been said, 'family and friends want a glimpse of God in the deceased's life and thus also in their own lives.'[25] The funeral homily, like the funeral itself, carries then the double task of speaking 'of the paschal mystery, as revealed in the suffering, death and resurrection of Jesus Christ, and simultaneously treating the experience of the dead person and the congregation,' who are the family and friends. Liturgical law has, in recent years, laid down that there is to be no eulogy and, because of this, some ministers have contented themselves with a brief word of sympathy to the sorrowing relatives. This, I would suggest, has robbed the liturgy of funerals of at least some of its purpose, depriving it of a sense of reality and failing to allow it to speak to the assembled gathering. Those min-

54

isters who have adopted this stance are not faced with any significant 'preaching' problem over the death of a parishioner by suicide! I would believe, however, that no matter how difficult it may seem, it is possible to marry successfully the two tasks of the homily in any funeral liturgy.

How do we speak of the dead?

How do we speak of the dead? Do we mention how they died, i.e., by suicide? Goodbyes are never easy and so we should not expect a funeral liturgy to be easy, but in the homily at the funeral of someone who has committed suicide, the minister can help the family say the 'goodbye' which they were not given the chance to say because of the suddenness of the death. The family need comfort and support and, with the community, they need to begin to understand what has happened to them. The experience of grievers wondering, 'is this all a nightmare?' is common. The funeral and the funeral homily must be real and must speak the language of death before the 'hope of resurrection' can mean anything to them. If we choose to speak of the dead person, (and I think we should) we need to remember that we are only taking a fleeting glimpse of that life through a little anecdote or segment that can demonstrate an affinity in some measure between the deceased and the Christian way of life or the life of Christ. The homily is not to be a eulogy, a speech in praise of a person's virtues or accomplishments but a little anecdote or glimpse into the deceased's life properly introduced can testify to the mystery of God's compassion and be a real source of comfort to the bereaved. In the case of a death by suicide, such an intervention during the homily can help the family to look, in their own time, for other instances in the life of the deceased where God's mercy and compassion were indeed clearly manifest. The minister may well, during the days of the wake, have searched out the most suitable incident by asking the family such questions as, 'How would you prefer to best remember …?' or 'What incident did yourself and … share, which brought you real peace and joy?' It is important that we do not 'canonise' a person in death whom we would not call a saint in life, and yet, obviously, we do not want to detail his faults or his failings. An easy balance is struck by a simple acknowledgement that 'like so many, he had his faults and failings.' Clearly, when recalling the positive, some selection will have to be made and the ability to taper the incident or the segment and still bring across the message will be an important deciding factor.

Do we mention suicide?
Do we mention suicide? Bernard Häring suggests:

> We should be most cautious in pronouncing the shocking word 'suicide'. Not only should we be aware of the legitimate limits of reductionism but also of the easily wounded sensitivity of relatives and friends. Faced with such a tragedy, we have to avoid any language that would seem to pass judgement.[26]

In the research for this project, none of the clergy interviewed mentioned the word 'suicide' in the homily. Most felt that it was in some way an 'improper' word to use on the occasion. Of the relatives who were interviewed, most were appreciative of the fact that the word 'suicide' wasn't used: 'I knew it was suicide alright but, at the time of the funeral, I just couldn't have coped with the word and all its implications.' Others who have attended funerals of suicides have appreciated the 'realness' of the liturgy. One typical comment made was, 'At least he didn't try to pretend it was a heart attack or an accident – he mightn't have used the word 'suicide' but he as much as did and I'm sure that was the right thing to do.'

The question still remains, 'Do we mention how the person died?' This is not an easy question for the minister to answer. He will want to consider a number of things. Firstly, is it certain that the person did, in fact, commit suicide and, if it is, how widely known is the fact? The minister should not consider that, because he is certain in his own mind or that because he has been told, that he has the right to confirm publicly that this is the case. Denial of death by suicide is a common phenomenon among families, even when the facts are clearly pointing to death by suicide – this may hinder their grief work but it should not be the minister 'from the pulpit' who faces them into the reality. A discussion with the family prior to the funeral will help the minister, and the decision to mention or not to mention the circumstances of the death should be taken in consultation with the family. One thing is fairly certain from the experience of many clergy: either way, the minister will certainly not satisfy everyone.

The pastoral minister will also ask himself how comfortable he is at dealing with the language of suicide and whether he might prefer to use expressions such as 'tragic death' or 'death in such difficult circumstances.' If it is agreed that the method of death be mentioned, then I suggest that it is much better to mention it as gently as possible in the opening introduction to the Mass. When it is clearly obvious that death was by suicide, to mention it at the start of Mass strikes an immediate note of realism into the gathering and touches the sentiment of both family and community and allows the liturgy to address the real situation, the real grief and the real suffering of the bereaved. It will, in my opinion, be imperative to stress that suicide is not an acceptable solution to problems, (it is dysfunctional behaviour; it is wrong) while at the same time avoiding any moral judgement of the person now deceased. Ministers should avoid the relatively easy categorising of the deceased as 'mentally ill' or as 'a sick person' – particularly if this wasn't clearly the case – since this has implications for others who are mentally ill and also raises the question of inherited mental illness for other members of the family. But the minister perhaps could talk about that moment or that short time when, 'no other answer seemed available to the deceased except suicide.'

Obviously the creation of a funeral homily amidst the pressures of other 'everyday' work is no easy task and perhaps the outline offered below might only serve to complicate the individual 'weaving pattern' by which each minister puts together 'the few words.' But it is offered here, not so much as a recipe, but rather as a list of possible ingredients.

A theological view

Robert A. Kreig, writing in *Worship,* May 1984, offers the following advice on funeral homilies in general :

> The aim of the funeral homily is to proclaim the mystery of God's love for us in Jesus Christ, as this is attested to in the liturgical texts and also in the life of the deceased. To accomplish this the homily is shaped by a dialectic between stories from the Bible and stories about the individual being buried.[27]

He offers the following outline for a funeral homily. (He considers the possibility of the person giving the homily being either male or female.)

(1) The Opening. An empathetic word is shared with the family and friends. The last days of the deceased are briefly recounted. The homilist states his or her two-fold aim: to recall God's gracious, though often strange ways, and to honour the one who has died.

(2) The congregation's sentiments. The homilist puts into words the swirl of thoughts, feelings and concerns of the congregation at the loss of the loved one. Ambiguities and dominant emotions are highlighted, for example, relief that the suffering is over, and yet pain and numbness at the separation.

(3) The readings. The sense of the readings is drawn out, especially as they express or contradict the sentiments of the congregation, and as they direct one's attention towards Jesus's suffering, death and resurrection.

(4) The deceased. A verbal portrait is given of the deceased. The homilist reviews the outline of his or her life, mentions the little things that typified the person, for example, a verbal expression, a hobby, a special place or person. Again the homilist recounts the individual's last days. Finally, he pinpoints a unifying dynamic, an element of the deceased's spirit, and considers how this quality flowed from the individual's response to God's invitation to life and love.

(5) The ending. The homilist reiterates the aim of his or her testimony, for example, to stand in wonder before God's way and to honour the deceased. The homilist exhorts the congregation to give thanks for the mystery of God's compassion and to do this even though the congregation may not understand much of this mystery.[28]

In their homilies at the funerals of those who had committed suicide, ministers have often raised the question of 'why', even though they realise that they will never be able to offer an answer. This is realistic because this is the question that is to the forefront of most people's minds. It is difficult to handle in the short time available and within the constraints of a homily but, as one priest put it, 'I think it is important for all to know that there are no easy answers and that you are at one with their struggle to find any answers at all.' Perhaps too it is important to alert the community to the complexities of the issue, not just so that they might understand but also because survivors have the right not to be blamed by society. Simple and often trite explanations can be the subject of 'neighbourhood gossip.' W. Guy Delaney, addresses the question thus:

> Why? This is the question we are all asking ourselves and one another. If we could only answer this question, somehow our grief might be more bearable, somehow our guilt might not rise up and accuse us so arrestingly, somehow the gloom that hangs over us like a starless night might be lifted. Why? It is so natural for us to ask the question, as if its answer could release us from the ache of John's death. But, my friends, the answer to this nagging question that goes on repeating itself in our thoughts and our conversations would not satisfy our heart's desire. To know why would solve very little. An answer would only give rise to the same question. No reason would be enough to set our minds at ease. No reason why would return the sparkle to our eyes and laughter to our voices.[29]

Sample Funeral Liturgy 1
for one who committed suicide

These liturgies incorporate some prayers from the Masses for the Dead contained in the Roman Missal. Many of these prayers are suitable for the occasion but some of them might require slight adaptation. Preparing for a funeral liturgy of one who has committed suicide should include pre-selecting the prayers of the Mass so that their tone and language is congruent with the reality of the suicide.

The Liturgies are presented here by way of example to illustrate the possibility of weaving together the themes from the readings, the sentiments of the congregation and the life and death of the deceased. They are not presented as 'standard' to be 'wheeled out' as the need arises and thus short-circuiting the very important process of planning and preparing the funeral liturgy in consultation with the bereaved family. It is hoped that no priest would use either as a 'ready-made' liturgy in his own parish.

Introduction and Penitential Rite

I welcome you all to our funeral Mass today. I welcome in particular (*name the immediate family of the deceased*). We have gathered with them to pray for the happy repose of the (*name the deceased*) who, in a time or moment of deep darkness and despair, tragically ended his own life. Though we know ourselves that this action is wrong in itself and that it is not an answer and does not provide a solution to any problem, we do not judge our brother (or sister) but commend him (her) to the mercy of God. For those who are bereaved our prayer too is heartfelt. The heavy burden of grief which you bear at this time will test your every resource; our prayer is that through faith and the compassion of God your hearts will be healed a little today and a little everyday until you can look forward to the great family re-union in God's kingdom.

You raise the dead to life in the Spirit.
Lord have mercy.
You bring pardon and peace to the sinner.
Christ have mercy.
You bring light to those in darkness.
Lord have mercy.

May almighty God have mercy on us,
forgive us our sins and bring us to everlasting life.

Let us pray:
God of mercy,
you are the hope of sinners
and the joy of saints.
We pray for our brother (N.)
whose body we honour with christian burial.
Give him happiness with your saints
and raise his body in glory at the last day
to be in your presence for ever. Amen.

or
God, lover of souls,
you hold dear what you have made
and spare all things, for they are yours.
Look gently on your servant N.,
and by the blood of the cross
forgive his/her failings.

Remember the faith of those who mourn,
and satisfy their longing for that day
when all will be made new again
in Christ, our risen Lord,
who lives and reigns with you for ever and ever. Amen.[30]

(Section 26, *Order of Christian Funerals*, Prayer 44, For one
who died by Suicide, in *Prayers and Psalms in Particular
Circumstances.*)

Headings for readings
First Reading: (Is 25:6-9) Death is part of life and mourning is part of living but God is our hope and our salvation and he alone will destroy the power of death and ease our pain and suffering.
Psalm: 129: Out of the depths I cry to you O Lord: We join with the psalmist and beg the Lord to come to us and hear our prayer.
Second Reading: (Rom 8: 31-35,37-39) In our sorrow and sadness we feel isolated and alone but God is with us in his Son Jesus Christ and he will stay with us in every trial and tribulation.
Gospel: (Mk 15:33-39; 16:1-6) Jesus, when faced with death, is fearful but entrusts himself to his Father's will and rises again and so triumphs over both fear and death.

Homily
We come today, my dear friends, to say farewell to (N) whose life has ended so suddenly and so tragically. Our sad farewell, with that of his nearest and dearest, is tinged with many questions about life and death, about living and dying, and about God and God's ways. I cannot possibly hope to find those answers for everyone today but with yourselves perhaps I can but briefly uncover where together we might start to search for some answers.

When someone so young chooses to end his life, we are inclined to wonder why, what led him to do it, what was on his mind, and to ask too, what will the result of this be, where will it end? We can only partly find answers to these questions and, in truth, maybe we will have to be satisfied with part answers.

The psalmist today recognises the depth of his affliction and from that depth he calls to the Lord to come to him, to hear him, to rescue him from all that is afflicting him. That too is where we start. We acknowledge to the Lord all our sorrows, our worries and our anxieties; we acknowledge too our doubts and our fears. If we are disappointed in a world that promised so much, or in life itself that seemed to have so much to offer and yet was so terribly fragile; or even if we are angry with ourselves or others or with the Lord himself, then we acknowledge all this and we ask the same Lord to be attentive to our pleading. And maybe the heavier our hearts are and the deeper our despair is, then the sharper our questions become – we do not hold them back from the Lord because, as St Paul tells us, 'neither death nor life, no angel, no prince, nothing that exists, nothing still to come, not any power, or height or depth, nor any created thing, can ever come between us and the love of God made visible in Christ Jesus our Lord.' We offer everything to the Lord, pouring ourselves out to him and then we listen, we listen to what he has to say. And today in our readings we hear God say that he will remove the mourning veil covering all the peoples, that he will destroy death forever. And he has done this and is doing this through the suffering, death and resurrection of his Son Jesus Christ on the cross. Jesus approached death with resoluteness and yet with trepidation, and when he died, the Gospel writer, perhaps lost for words to describe the agony, the grief and the hopelessness of his loved ones, his mother and the disciples, simply says, 'The veil of the temple was torn in two from top to bottom.' And yet through his death on the cross and his glorious resurrection, Jesus conquered for all time the power of death. He removed from it, not the effects of loss and grief that it inflicts on mourners, but most certainly the sting of finality that it brought to the dead. Be assured your loved-one lives.

(Here the preacher might then refer to some incident, aspect or quality of the deceased's life that indicated his love of life and of his faith and/or of his religious practice.)

Today our final farewell to (N) affords us the opportunity to give thanks to God for his generosity in affording a merciful judgement on all those who have died, and to ask the Lord to reach out in tenderness and compassion to those who mourn today, to *(name the chief mourners)* with whom we sympathise. We pledge ourselves to continue to remember, in the days and weeks and months ahead, them and their loss and their sorrow until their hearts are healed and their mourning resting, and they find peace in the risen Lord.

Prayer of the Faithful
Because it is likely that some relatives and friends will be reading individual prayers of the faithful, I have chosen to exclude any mention of suicide from them. However, the priest himself might like to add some prayers and I include some possibilities at the end.

Priest: God Our Father, when your Son was dying on Calvary you heard his heartfelt plea. Hear today our prayers for (N) who has died and for his sorrowing family and friends.

1. We pray for (N) who has died. May he find rest in the peace of your kingdom. Lord hear us.

2. We pray for the family and friends of (N). May they be comforted and strengthened in their tragic loss by the love of God, shown to them in the depth of their own faith and the continued support of the community. Lord hear us.

3. We pray for all of us gathered here today, that we may free ourselves from rash judgement, work to support the weaker members of our community, and trust in the Lord always. Lord hear Us.

4. We pray for all those who have died, especially those who were close to us and dear to us, that God may reward them with eternal life. Lord hear us.

God our Father, nothing can ever come between us and the love of God. Receive our brother (N) into your heavenly kingdom to be at peace with Jesus Christ your Son, and grant our earthly petitions through the same Christ our Saviour. Amen.

Some alternatives
1. We pray for our brother (N) who has taken his own life. We pray that he will find the peace and rest which he longed for in this life and that he will rise again on the last day with no more sorrow. Lord hear us.
2. We pray for all who may consider taking their own lives, that they may receive the help they need and recognise other answers to their problems and be strengthened to face the uncertainties of this life. Lord hear us.
3. We pray that this tragic ending to (N)'s life may not let us forget the good which he did. Particularly we remember and thank God for (*here mention the involvement of the deceased in his family or in some community enterprise*). Lord hear us.

Funeral Liturgy 2
for one who committed suicide

Introduction and Penitential Rite

We gather today, my dear friends, to bid farewell to (N) whose sudden and untimely death has left his sorrowing family and friends shocked, numb and deeply wounded. I welcome them to this Mass, especially (*here mention the names of the close relatives*) and I invite them to offer their grief, their sorrow, with their prayers, to Almighty God. Together we will offer this Mass for the happy repose of (N) and for healing and comfort to come to these his loved ones.

Lord Jesus, you gave your life that we might live for ever.
Lord have mercy.
Lord Jesus, you comfort us in all our sorrows.
Christ, have mercy.
Lord Jesus, you will come again to take us to yourself.
Lord have mercy.
(*Penitential Rite* taken from *Christian Burial*)

Let us pray:
Almighty God and Father of all,
you strengthen us by the mystery of the cross
and with the sacrament of your Son's resurrection.
Have mercy on our brother/sister N..
Forgive all his/her sins and grant him/her peace.
May we who mourn this sudden death be comforted
and consoled by your power and protection.
We ask this through Christ our Lord. Amen[31]
(Prayer 45 from *Prayers and Psalms in Particular Circumstances*, Section 26, *Order of Christian Funerals*)

Headings for readings
First Reading: (Lam : 3:17-26) Faced with deep pervading unhappiness, anguish and affliction, the writer remembers that the favours of the Lord are not all past and his kindnesses are never exhausted.
Psalm: (Ps 102:8,10,13-18) God, our loving Father, looks with pity on all his children who are in need.
Second Reading: (1 Jn 3:1-2) In the kingdom to come, we shall be like God because we shall see him as he really is.
Gospel Reading: (Jn 14:1-6) We are urged that, no matter what, we should trust in God and know that there are places in abundance in his kingdom.

Homily
My dear friends, Jesus is gathered with his disciples to celebrate with them a religious meal, the annual passover meal. Traditionally this was a sacred and yet a joyous celebration, but on this occasion, which we have now come to call the Last Supper, Jesus begins to prepare his disciples for his departure from them. He tells them that he will be leaving them and he immediately senses their sadness and sorrow at his going and so he assures them: 'Do not let your hearts be troubled. Trust in God still and trust in me. There are many rooms in my Father's house.' Jesus was a realist. He knew he could not prevent, nor would he have wanted to prevent, their sorrowing after him, but he did want to leave them a farewell gift, something they could hold on to; something solid which would steady them and something that would give them hope when he didn't seem to be near to them. Essential to this were the sayings: 'Trust in God still,' 'Trust in me,' and 'There are many rooms in my Father's house and I am going to prepare you a place.'

Today Jesus offers that very same gift to this sorrowing family: 'Trust in God still. Trust in me. There are many rooms in my Father's house ... and I am going to prepare you a place.' Your loved one (N) has ended his own life. He chose to do so at that moment of despair, of hopelessness or helplessness, or at that moment of imbalance when no other solution seemed open to him. And though of itself we know the act of suicide[32] is wrong, we do not condemn (N) for the choice he made, for the action which he committed. We do not condemn because we do not know and we cannot know the depth of his pain, his anguish or his mental suffering. But more than this, we do not condemn because what we do know, and what we constantly need to remind ourselves of, is in the words of today's psalm: 'The Lord is compassion and love, slow to anger, rich in mercy. He does not treat us according to our sins, nor repay us according to our faults.' And so it is to the mercy and compassion of God that we commend (N). And when, in the days and weeks to come, we wonder at where his soul might be resting, we will surely be comforted by the gift of those words of Jesus himself: 'In my Father's house there are many rooms and I am going now to prepare a place for you.'

It is difficult today, and it will be difficult for many days to come, to trust in God still and to trust in his Son Jesus Christ. Yet I invite you to cling to that trust. Remember today not just the death of (N) but remember his life – remember the good times (*here mention the good characteristics etc. of the deceased*). Today, like the writer of the Book of Lamentations, your souls are shut out from peace, your strength is gone and your spirits have sunk within you. Today, like those disappointed disciples who shared the Last Supper with Jesus, you now stand on a Calvary Hill that is all your own. Gaze there on the wretched, torn, dying and dead body of Jesus and then search for the gift of his words, to be for you a strength in your sorrow and grief. By his suffering and his death, by his glorious resurrection, Jesus Christ did indeed prepare a place in the kingdom of heaven for all his people. He offers it to each one, robbing death of its terrible power over them. No longer will death be the end, but it will be a beginning; a beginning for what, we might well ask, and the first letter of St John puts its well: 'My dear people, we are already the children of God, but what we are to be in the future has not yet been revealed; all we know is that when it is revealed, we shall be like him because we shall see him as he really is.'

Today our prayer is that the place prepared by Jesus Christ for (N) is being offered to him and that he, who through his baptism was called a child of God, having been forgiven whatever sins were his, through human frailty, is now seeing God as he really is. Our prayer too is that those who are left with the burden of anguish will find, on this earth, that the healing hand of Jesus is stretched out to them, who in their saddest moments trusted in God still and in his Son Jesus Christ.

Prayer of The Faithful
Because it is likely that some relatives and friends will be reading the individual Prayers of the Faithful, I have chosen to exclude any mention of suicide from them. However, the priest himself might prefer to add some prayers and I include some possibilities at the end.

Priest: God our Father, you have told us to trust in you always and so, in our grief and mourning, we come to you in prayer.

1. We pray for (N) whose life has ended so suddenly and tragically. We commend him to your mercy and compassion. Lord hear us.

2. We pray for this sorrowing family who today bid farewell to their loved one (N). Comfort them in their grief and strengthen them to face life again with renewed hope. Lord hear us.

3. We pray for all those who are burdened with worries, anxieties and problems for which they can find no answers. May they find comfort in their faith and reach out so that they can be supported by their family and community. Lord hear us.

4. We pray for the congregation who gather here today to mourn (N's) death and to bid him farewell. May we remember the good in life which he did and may we continue to support his loved ones in their loss. Lord hear us.

Priest: God our Father, look now with compassion on your people; touch their troubled hearts with kindnesses new, and sustain them with the promise of eternal life for (N). And may we all look forward to being reunited with our loved ones in the peace and happiness of your kingdom. We ask this through Christ our Lord. Amen.

Some alternatives

1. We pray for (N) who has died so suddenly and so tragically and by his own hand. We pray that the darkness, the despair and the depression which he experienced will now be replaced by light, contentment and peace in the kingdom of the Lord. Lord hear us.

2. We pray for all who are lost at this time in their unhappy world, particularly those who may be considering taking their own lives. May they be strengthened in their faith, find the support and help they need within the community and live life to its fullness. Lord hear us.

3. We pray that we will remember (N), not just because of the tragic ending to his life, but most especially for the good which he did (*here mention the good works with which the deceased was associated*). As we thank God for that good, we pray that it will have helped him on his journey to salvation. Lord hear us.

PART IV

Ongoing grief ministry

> *Blessed are those who mourn:*
> *They shall be comforted.*
> (Mt 5:5)

To such shock and grief the pastoral care provider brings resources available nowhere else. To hear that God is still powerfully present with understanding, compassion and hope amid encircling gloom, is very likely the margin of difference for healing so terribly wounded a soul. That assurance is likely to be best communicated through the earthen vessel of a truly empathetic pastoral ministry. Such ministry incorporates both the essentials of deep compassion and the confidence of rational meaning behind some agonising variables of the universe. These essentials are communicated best in simple ways. In quietness will be our strength. Calm presence speaks powerfully. Those who believe fervently in the indwelling of Christ bring not only themselves but the focussed presence of God's continuing incarnation. That incarnation imparts the message of life over death. It affirms that though we die, yet shall we live. No greater comfort or consolation can be offered the grieving heart that is suffering the loss of a loved one.[33]

'They were very good at the time, but they never came back.' 'I needed them, not to tell me anything, but just to be here – and they weren't.' In my research for this project, I discovered some very bitter 'kith and kin' of those who had committed suicide. Many of them told of how good the Church, through the priests, had been to them at the time of death, but how hurt they felt and how let down they felt by the lack of support in the days, weeks and months after the funeral. It is perhaps an understatement that priests take death very much for granted in the community and recognise the bereavement-coping mechanisms and support-structures that exist naturally and at a very ordinary level within families and communities. But in more recent times it is recognised that the bereaved need help and support and that the circumstances of some bereavements require some very definite and purposeful extra help and support. Bereavement through the death of a loved one by suicide is certainly one such case. (In these notes I will presume that the grief support is being given by a priest, but it may well be that this ministry is shared with other members of the faithful, and in particular the ministry might include the idea of like-to-like ministry within support groups or on an individual basis.)

I can readily understand why a minister might shy away from involvement with the bereaved – it is an area that will demand a tremendous investment of spiritual and emotional energy as well as time in ongoing visits. In short, it involves a high level of priestly commitment, often on a one-to-one basis or on a ·priest-to-family basis. It is not easy work and, when the death has been as the result of a suicide, it can be a slow, painful, uphill struggle for a long time. Those who would take on this work are advised to enter it with great patience and prayer and the support of prayer friends within the community. The initial entry-experiences of even the most experienced bereavement-counsellors have been that of being almost thrown by the 'overwhelming confusion, denial and anger' at this death by suicide. The walls of protection that are thrown around the family can be high and forbidding, and yet, within the family, the increase in emotional outbursts and dysfunctional behaviour call for the intervention of loving and caring 'outsiders.'

What are the qualities necessary to bring to grief ministry? Are there any special qualities needed because the death was by suicide?

A portrait of a healing minister
Donna Reilly Williams and JoAnn Sturzl offer the following portrait of a healing minister:

(1) *A genuine love for the other.* This is a non-possessive love, which accepts others just as they are and desires the best for them. If you do not truly love the other in this sense, you will probably not be able to help. When this kind of love is in action, God is at work.
(2) *A non-judgemental attitude.* The person to whom you minister may not share your moral standards, values or behaviour. But this is the other person's lived experience, and it is from this reality that the mourner will journey. You are not there to condemn, but to

help. Your stance is to want what is good for the other and to assist the person in moving through the pain.

(3) *Faith in the other.* With this attitude, a minister believes that hurting people have within themselves all that is needed to solve their problems, all that is needed to discover the steps toward peace and wholeness. Each person has an inner life; the Spirit of God lives within everyone. You can help others discover their own faith and liberate the life and resources within them.

Faith in the other has a positive effect on growth and change. Jesus empowered and transformed people. When he met the woman at the well, he saw beyond her identity as a woman and as a Samaritan. He revealed God's promise to her as well as his identity as Messiah. She was then empowered to tell this 'good news' to others.

The woman put down her water jar and hurried back to the town to tell the people, 'Come and see a man who has told me everything I have done, could this be the Christ?' (Jn 4:28-29)

(4) *Genuineness and honesty.* Living this attitude means both to be aware of your inner reality (including feelings) and to express this inner reality honestly and clearly. This means that if you do not understand the experience or values of the person you are ministering to, do not pretend that you do. Genuine caregivers communicate both a deep interest in understanding and an honesty about the struggle.

Being in the presence of someone who is honest and true enables those who mourn to enter their own truth.
(*Grief Ministry*, pp. 89 and 90).

When it comes to ministering to families who have experienced bereavement because of a suicide, perhaps some practical points might be offered.

People do get stuck
Erich Lindemann and Ina May Greer, both pioneers in the modern study of grief, say:

> The survivors of a suicide are likely to get 'stuck' in their grieving and to go on for years in a state of cold isolation, unable to feel close to others and carrying always with them the feeling that they are set apart or under the threat of doom.[34]

Grievers need tremendous space, space to be questioning, space to be angry with themselves, with the suicide victim, with the community and with God. They need space to express complicated emotions that will very often include guilt (the 'if only I had:' syndrome) and to include denial ('It must have been an accident.') They will want to blame all kinds of people, agencies and circumstances:

> Perhaps it is the anger, that basic crude emotion, that is the most difficult to express and the most piercing to hear, that locks so many survivors for years in their cold isolation. Even in families that share many private feelings, expressing anger at the deceased meets resistance.[35]

The caregiver must be prepared to be in this 'lions cage' with the griever, helping them to verbalise even the 'most unreasonable' feelings. The caregiver must assure the griever that there are no right or wrong ways to react to their loss and that no feeling should be denied an airing in the confidentiality of this one-to-one situation.

Don't be a fixer

Carers needs to recognise that they do not have to fix things up for people; the need to assure people that 'this was not the case' or to defend the accused – 'Do you really think God would have done that on you?' – these temptations need to be resisted. Carers should not offer answers but help people find their own answers, knowing that a person's own experience of what things mean is usually self-corrective if it is allowed to be, and that ultimately people will find the only acceptable and relevant answers themselves.

Good listener

Carers need to be good listeners, helping people talk and recognising the non-verbal clues that might give indications of areas that need to be talked out. As time progresses, the carer should be able to see the griever slowly move through grief work; if it appears that this is not happening, it might be well to suggest the introduction of some professional help. The idea of 'family-ministry' might well be appealing to the priest, whereby he is able to facilitate individuals sharing within the family circle of his or her thoughts, feelings and emotions so enabling progress in their grief work. This can be also very helpful as stories of pleasant memories as well as of unpleasant memories of the deceased are shared. Survivors can often be supported by attending a support-group to such an extent that they themselves can eventually become carers.

Why?

In the case of death by suicide, the inevitable 'why' will be a question that survivors will continue to ask time and time again. The caregiver should realise that there will not be a satisfactory answer to this question. However, he should not dissuade the survivors from asking the question and seeking the answers. The caregiver needs to remember that it is not *his* bereavement nor grief and it is not *his* place to establish what questions should or should not be asked. Iris Bolton has this to say to survivors:

> You will ask 'why' a million times and you need to ask the question. You may never know the complete answer of why, but it's important to struggle with the question. Then one day you will be able to let it go and not need to know anymore. Then you will be dealing with how to go on with your lives. The meaning I have found in my own son's suicide is to realise that life is tenuous for us all, so I have the choice of making every minute count with my family from now on and valuing them and friends and life in a way I never did before.[36]

Some bargains

Christopher Lukas and Henry M. Seiden, in their book, *Silent Grief, Living in the Wake of Suicide,*[37] identify some of the things that survivors do to deal with suicide. These they call bargains.

> Bargains allow survivors to be a little more comfortable with their survivorship. Bargains enable survivors to go on living. We call them bargains because there is a trade-off involved in these deals. The survivor gives up something in return for a more comfortable emotional position. The survivor pays a price and gets something in return. Bargains protect survivors against feelings or thoughts that are too painful to deal with. But they also lead survivors into behaviour that is harmful to them.[38]

What are these bargains? Here is a list of the principal bargains identified by Lukas and Seiden with a brief explanation of each.

Scapegoating: The survivor finds one or more people who he or she believes are responsible for the death of the person who actually killed himself. By focusing on the scapegoat, the survivor avoids having to deal with any anger that might have been felt at themselves or at the person who committed suicide.

The long good-bye: Suicide is usually a sudden death with no opportunity to say goodbye. The bargain of fruitlessly trying to say goodbye is that, if you are still doing this, then the person isn't gone yet and you don't have to experience, at least not fully, the loss of that person.

I am guilty: After suicide one of the overwhelming feelings that survivors experience is guilt; struggling with this is part of their grief work. But if they don't fight this sense of guilt and then begin to accept that they are in fact not guilty, they need never face any anger that they might have experienced, particularly anger at the deceased.

Cutting off: In this bargain, survivors cut themselves or some part of themselves off from life. Usually, as a punishment, they do not allow themselves to experience ever again anything good in life, either a good time or good relationships or the freedom to experience and to share their feelings. Here the drive may well be to get on with living at an acceptable level, but the price is the refusal to bring your full self to that living.

Because you died, I'll die: Most survivors of suicide experience at least some impulse to commit suicide themselves. It can become for them an overriding fear and nightmare; in the midst of their overwhelming pain and suffering, suicide may become an option, made legitimate for them through the death by suicide of the one for whom they grieve.

Silence: Here the bargain can be made within a family not to talk to anyone about the suicide. This can provide the unity that a family feels they need against what they perceive to be the accusatory limelight in which they find themselves within the community. The silence also prevents the verbalising of any anger, guilt or blame and creates an atmosphere of seeming calmness and congeniality. However, those caught up in this great bargain are deprived of the opportunity of personal grief work and this will take its toll on the lives and the personalities of all involved.

The carer, duly warned, perhaps then can interrupt and break the bargain, creating an opportunity for positive grief work among the bereaved. It may be that he will recognise that a more professional helper is needed to cope with this complication and be able to introduce same.

Grief and bereavement theory

There has been considerable research into the process of recovery from grief, much of this pioneered by Erich Lindemann, an American psychiatrist/psychologistappointedbytheUnitedStates Govern-ment to tend to the 'psychiatric sequellae of the Coconut Grove Fire in Boston in 1942.' Lindemann[39] identified grief work, the process by which a person must proceed during grieving, as having three distinct aspects, namely: (1) emancipation from the bondage to the deceased; (2) readjustment to the environment in which the deceased is missing; (3) the formation of new relation-ships. When these aspects were spelt out in more concrete terms they resembled very much the stage process identified by Dr Elizabeth Kübler-Ross[40] marking emotional milestones in a dying patient's journey toward death. Kübler-Ross had rightly observed that, by acknowledging the journey and its milestones, a person could be facilitated through that journey. An altogether too rigid application of this theory has resulted in some considerable stress for dying patients and their relatives – when their emotional needs and reactions didn't fit the norm, the question might then be posed, what were they doing wrong? Similarly the attempt to define grief as a stage-process has led to many inexperienced counsellors and carers attempting to stage-manage someone else's grief. 'Grief is the emotional, spiritual and physical response to the loss of some-one or something in whom or in which one had been strongly invested.' When we consider the number of variables in this defi-nition, we begin to realise that individuals will chart their own course on the grief journey; for some, certain parts will be more difficult than others. Those who would help must allow the griev-ing person the time needed but also be available to help those who might get stuck in one part or another.

In this section I will offer three of the principal ways of viewing grief: as a process, as a series of tasks and as a transition.

Each of them, in my opinion, offers valuable insights to the carer but none of them can be of assistance if it is used to establish expectations of a route through which a griever *has to pass* during grief work. These theories can only illuminate and help to give meaning to the journey through grief taken by the bereaved person at his own pace and in his own way.[41]

Bereavement as a process
Theorists believe that the griever passes through a number of phases. Before looking at these phases, it is important to realise that they are not neat compartments which follow on from each other. They are rather helps to analyse where people may be in the grieving process and it is important to note that people may move forward and backwards until their grieving is done.

Phase 1: Here the griever experiences shock, numbness and the pain of grief. During this the person may emotionally over-react (excessive crying, screaming or fainting) or under-react (coldness, distancing oneself, over-composed). The shock and numbness provides a framework within which a person can cope with visitors, funeral arrangements and the actual burial. Only when the numbness begins to wear off will the person begin to experience the intensity of loss and begin to come to terms with it.

Phase 2: Here the griever experiences within himself a complex web of emotions and feelings including fear, guilt, anger and resentment. The fear is often over what the future holds of how will he cope even with small things. The guilt can be from some unresolved conflict with the one deceased or can be what has become known as survivor-guilt – why should I be living when my loved one is dead? The anger can be against oneself, or against the deceased (particularly if the death was by suicide) or against doctors or nurses (who mustn't have done enough). It can also be against God. The resentment can be against one's nearest and dearest who don't have to experience this – their loved one (partner or child or parent) is still living! Helping the grievers cope with and verbalise such a catharsis of feelings will help them progress through their grief work.

Phase 3: Grievers are unable to engage themselves in the pattern of life which they had previously experienced and shared in; even doing ordinary everyday things is considered a burden and heavy chore. Their life is characterised by disinterest, apathy and an unwillingness to plan even the most ordinary everyday things. This phase might well be called the 'sad phase' because the person constantly dwells on the sad events which have happened but without the high level of emotional reaction which characterised the previous phase.

Phase 4: This is the positive phase of letting go of the past and moving towards the future. However it must be stressed that it is a very gradual thing; the past is not one big block that is suddenly set aside. Rather a person begins to leave some elements of the past behind and replace them slowly with new patterns of living and it is only then that the healing takes place.

Bereavement as a series of tasks

Here the theorists view bereavement almost as a challenge to the person to move through a set of tasks. This theory sees recovery from bereavement as a 'process of reconstruction, with new rules, different boundaries, changing relationships and some new behaviours.'[42] Its advantage as theory is that it openly permits and encourages the bereaved to control the pace of their adjustment and to invite outside help at any stage.

Task 1: To accept the reality of the loss. The bereaved person must face the fact that the deceased is dead and that this situation is irreversible. People in their bereavement can be helped in many ways to accept this fact. Funeral rites, like viewing the body and being present at the committal, can contribute here. On the other hand, there are death-denying practices that are becoming more widespread and these include the use of euphemism, like 'passed away' or 'gone to heaven'.

Task 2: To experience pain and grief. Today's world is a cushioning world with many pain-relieving drugs and distractions. The person bereaved must be allowed to, and be able to, experience the full painful extent of his loss.

Task 3: To adjust to a new environment. A person has died and so, for those who are left, all the roles that the deceased played in their lives are now missing; a reflection on these roles will be part of the task of experiencing the real pain of the loss. Adjusting to being without the person who fulfilled these roles might simply mean being on one's own for longer times or doing things oneself, or allowing others to do them. Adjusting to the new environment may well call for many changes to previously established patterns of living.

Task 4: To withdraw emotional energy and re-invest it in other relationships. This for many people will be the most difficult task because thoughts of 'betrayal' of the deceased will arise naturally. This task then will be undertaken slowly and sometimes almost unconsciously.

Bereavement as a transition
In this theory, the death of a loved one is seen as a change, albeit a major change, through which a person has to move. It is believed that the experience of any transition or change requires similar coping skills and that the identification and the development of such skills will help people in their grief work. The coping skills centre on the person and are initiated and implemented from within the person's self in a stage-process similar to the phase theory of bereavement.

Stage 1: Immobilisation. When faced with severe stress, the mind shuts off. This is particularly acute when the stress was unanticipated, like the news of a sudden death. The person does not have to deal with the emotional turmoil that such news may bring; he may go into shut-out where it is very difficult (or even impossible) to communicate with him, or he may remain quite calm, attending to all the practical implications, but not to any of the emotional ones.

Stage 2: Minimisation. Here the person tries to minimise the importance of the event or the impact of the event – 'At least it wasn't as bad as it might have been,' or, 'wouldn't you have hated it to be like it was for such and such a person?'

Stage 3: Depression. Here the person begins to realise the finality of the death and is overcome with sadness.

Stage 4: Acceptance of reality. Here the loss is accepted fully and this marks the beginning of the possibility of new growth.

Stage 5: Testing. Here the person explores himself and how he copes in the different situation now that his loved one has gone.

Stage 6: Search for Meaning. There is a continuing search

for some personal meaning in the tragedy of the loved one's death. People need to be able to put their own meaning on the death before they can agree with themselves to live with it.

Stage 7: Internalisation. This is the final stage of the transition process, when the person has been able to give expression and meaning to his experience and to adjust his attitudes and way of life to the changed circumstances in which he finds himself.

Helping children to grieve

I include this section 'Helping children to grieve' and the section, 'Supporting teenagers and young people following suicide,' because I consider that these are two areas that may require special intervention from the pastoral minister. I am conscious that situations differ greatly and that the age of the children and the traumatised state of the parent or parents are clearly important factors in how children can or will be helped in their grieving. It isn't possible in this short section to consider fully the help that children need in grieving and so what follows are only general guidelines to enable ministers and parents to help children to grieve.

There is a very natural protective instinct in adults, particularly in parents, to shield children from unpleasantness and upset. Death is one of the occasions when this instinct to protect and to cushion, if misdirected, can have very long-term devastating effects on a child's development. If that protectiveness includes a game of make-believe, that everything is alright, that they are just going away to their cousins for a few days, then a parent or parents may be building up for themselves a situation where their child will never again trust or believe them, and the death of their loved one will be but the marker for the start of many years of unhappiness and discord in that family. Parents, wishing to protect their children from the reality of death, are often supported by other adults who themselves might find it difficult to cope with children in the grieving situation. The minister, observing the situation, may well be the only one in a trusted position to intervene on behalf of the immediate welfare and the future well-being of the children. Parents may indeed seek and welcome the advice of the minister in the situation.

Children know grief

Children have from their earliest days learned grief, for example, the pain of separation when their mother put them into the cradle or went away and left them for a short time with someone else. Grief is part of their learned experience. Children have the same emotional needs after the death of their loved one as adults do, and yet they are often ignored by those who would sympathise with grieving adults. The pastoral minister can give a lead in this matter, expressing sympathy, both at the home of the deceased and publicly at the funeral, with the grieving children as well as with the adults. The children may not have learned the social graces or customary ways of responding but nevertheless they do experience the need to be comforted.

The truth

When someone close to them dies, children should be told the truth. The words, 'die,' 'death' and 'dead' may seem hard words to use to children, but they are preferable words to 'gone' or 'taken away' or 'asleep' or 'gone to heaven,' because for a child these latter words have a sense of a condition that is not permanent and can be reversed. It may be necessary to explain to a child what 'being dead' means – the dead don't breathe, they feel nothing, they cannot see or hear, they no longer move or speak or smile; they are cold, their bodies have stopped working. The permanence of death is very hard for a child to grasp and it will be this that the child will struggle with most. Parents or surviving adults should be encouraged to share with the child how they too are struggling with the permanence of death and that their feelings are mixed.

> Until (children) are quite sure a person is no more, and will never be, they cannot finish the work of mourning. And if they cannot finish it, they cannot free themselves to go on with life and love and growing ... A family can trade all kinds of memories together, pulling out snapshots, laughing over funny times and times that made them angry too, talking over fights as well as fun ... Then a child can live the death like a story he is part of ... And when the story is remembered well, fully felt and finished, a child can go on to turn new pages in his life.[43]

Be honest with children

Pastoral ministers can encourage parents to be honest with their children about how the person died and the cause of death. If the death was from suicide, the children should be told what has happened, in terms that they recognise. One mother said, 'I told my little boy on the day before he made his First Holy Communion. I felt he deserved to know what had happened. Also I felt that he needed to know that he was in no way responsible for his daddy's death.'

It was not God's will!

Ministers can ask parents not to use 'God' or 'God's will' to explain death to children. Adults readily use the expression 'God's will' and have explored for themselves the depth of connotation associated with the expression. A child's idea of God as a loving Father can be exploded immediately by saying such things as, 'God must have needed her more than we did,' or 'God must have his reason for this,' or 'It's God's holy will.' The child then begins to see God as the big all-powerful bully who is to blame for this death.

Spending time and listening

Ministers can encourage parents to spend time with their children and listen to their children's questions, particularly in the days immediately after death. There is tremendous pressure on grieving adults to be present to meet those who call and to leave their children in the hands of someone else. Grieving children need their parents, particularly if it is a surviving parent. They have immediate questions to ask and sometimes strong feelings, creating in them a deep sense of insecurity. Parents should answer the children's questions with the truth when it is known and should encourage children to ask all their questions. Parents sometimes fear this questioning by their children and the pastoral minister can often help by encouraging the parent or by being present with the family. One parent, worried for five years as to whether her son, now aged fifteen, knew how his dad had died and if he didn't, how would she tell him that it was suicide? She used the occasion of the researcher's visit to ask her son, only to discover that he had known from the morning the body had been found. They might have supported each other better in their trauma had the truth been openly shared at the time.

Unspoken feelings

Ministers can encourage parents to address their child's unspoken feelings. The minister is often quick to spot how children, unable to express verbally the complexity or magnitude of their feelings, act these out in misbehaviour or in incongruent behaviour (weeping one minute, laughing the next), or play, or in long periods of silence. By pointing out to parents this behaviour, and suggesting how they might talk through these feelings with the children, the pastoral minister can indirectly minister to the children in a more successful way than through any contrived chats between the child and the minister himself. Sadness and fear for the future are usually the most deep-rooted feelings experienced by a child during a time of grief. Doubts and worries, too, may have arisen in their young minds from things they have overheard. This alerts us to the foolishness of telling children lies in relation to death but especially to a death by suicide – they will pick up information from other sources and recognise deception. It is my firm opinion that those in ministry should never be party to child grievers being deceived, however well meaning the deception is.

Freedom to talk

Ministers can encourage parents and others to encourage children to talk about the deceased. Particularly in the case of death by suicide, the freedom to talk about the deceased will help children realise that the death wasn't their fault – it is not uncommon for children to blame themselves for the death, especially when there may have been even a minor unpleasantness or an unresolved row between the child and the deceased or when the child may have wished (even privately) ill-fortune or even death on the person now deceased. By talking about the deceased, children can be helped release themselves from any sense of blame. They are also encouraged to avoid another real block to their recovery, that of 'denial,' – the person is not really dead. In the case of death by suicide, children will be confused if the deceased is scapegoated or overly praised. It will be necessary both to seek a balance in the discussion and also to discuss with the children better ways of handling problems other than by suicide.

Shame

In the case of a death by suicide of a loved one, children very often feel deeply shamed, particularly when they return to school. Other children can say things, which they may have picked up in their own home, about the person who committed suicide or about the circumstances of the death; the bereaved child is particularly vulnerable to ridicule. The child coping with loss may need additional help to overcome the sense of shame that he or she feels the suicide has brought on them.

Prayer in school

In the aftercare of mourners, it is all too easy to forget about the bereaved child. A little prayer service in the child's classroom at school and the pastoral minister's presence at a family conference or family prayers can be of assistance.

Supporting young people following a suicide

I have borrowed the title of this section, 'Supporting young people following a suicide,' from the literature of the Minnesota Extension Service, based at the University of Minnesota and under the general heading 'Teens in Distress'. Some may wonder why select 'young people' for a special section, why not wives or husbands or parents, and the point is debatable. I have no doubt that each group has its own special needs and indeed that each individual, grieving loss by suicide, is unique and his grief and sense of loss unique, and therefore his needs unique as well. However suicide among younger people is an increasing phenomenon and, with that, there are increasing numbers of young people having to cope, at a very difficult time in their lives, with the loss through death by suicide of a brother or sister, a close friend or a school mate. With every suicide, but particularly with the suicide of a young person, there is an increased fear, and not without good reason, among the entire community of the 'copycat' phenomenon whereby other young people will attempt to end their problems by ending their lives. It is to help pastoral ministers to be aware of and to address these factors that I include this special section on supporting young people following a suicide.

Iris Bolton recounts how she spoke to a High School audience about grief and mourning the day after one of their number, Randy, had been buried. He had shot himself:

> ... many students felt guilty and were angry with themselves for feeling guilty. 'How can I be angry at a dead friend? But I am!' exclaimed a 15-year-old boy. I had learned that kids were turning their anger toward God, their friends, their teachers and their parents. Some spoke

of wanting to end their own lives in this unfair world. I spoke calmly, touching on all that I had learned about the shock of suicide and recovery from the terrible pain ... I spoke to the kids as if they were adults. I told them that guilt was natural and anger was natural, indeed necessary. I told them that the worst thing that could happen now was that they might hide from themselves. 'So talk about Randy,' I urged, 'Talk to each other and to your parents. Some of you may want to cling to your guilt until it turns to hate. If you do, it will deform you. I have a thing about guilt. I say, if you feel guilty, feel guilty. Get into it. Feel it until you're tired of it. If you feel mad, feel mad. If you feel sad, feel sad. I mean, get into it hard. And do it all with no self-judgement, no self-blame.' They listened intently.

'If you feel guilt, it's because you are normal and human. But if you choose to hold onto that feeling forever you may need to ask yourself why you need to stay there. Are you punishing yourself for something that's real? Sometimes it feels like you're saying, 'If I don't feel rotten, it's like I'm betraying Randy's memory.' But by hanging onto your self-punishment, you may turn mourning into a life-style that can produce a twisted human being.'

I urged, 'Most of all don't deny your feelings. What you deny acquires enormous power over your life. Those things that you push back into your mind, like the word suicide, for instance, pile up inside you, and when the pile is big enough it may explode.

'I believe that the things you don't deal with openly, fester and swell until they acquire enough power to control your life.

'The point is that if you feel something, even if it's negative, lay it out on the table, and look at it. Then you may eventually get tired of it, and then you can let it go.

'It's natural to agonise over Randy's death,' I concluded, 'but don't stay silent. Talk about the crazy things he did, the good things, the bad things. He was a human being like yourselves, trying to find himself. Yesterday we buried him in Arlington Cemetery, but don't try to bury him in the back of our minds. Keep him up front because he was part of your life and a part of your learning experience in this high school. So honour him by speaking his name.' I spoke for thirty minutes ...[44]

The paStoral minister is usually the leader in the community who will be making the first public reference to the suicide, usually at the funeral of the deceased. It may also be his duty to lead a memorial service in the school where the young person or the young person's brothers and sisters attend. Experts in the field of preventing suicide believe that proper postvention, the support given to survivors, is essentially prevention, especially when it comes to dealing with young people as survivors who are potentially suicide's next victims. There are many approaches but it is generally agreed that community leaders, parents, teachers, youth leaders and clergy should address six areas and I will here treat of each separately :

A troubled personality
Stress the fact that suicide is the result of a troubled personality. It is dysfunctional behaviour. Here it is important to convey to young people that suicide is neither a common nor an acceptable way for healthy people to deal with their problems, whether these arise from stress, loss, conflict or depression. Those who have used suicide must have been deeply troubled and unable to deal with the present or face the future; their hopelessness, despair and pain must have been tremendous and, because of that, they did not have the resources to see the alternatives. This person chose the dysfunctional way, but there are other ways, healthy ways, constructive ways and successful ways of dealing with problems and stresses. Young people need to be reassured that these other ways are available and do work .

Don't identify with ...
Reduce identification with the actions of the deceased – it was his action, not someone else's fault. The young people who were friends of the deceased are truly 'chief mourners' and they need the attention of the minister in the same kind of way. Often they identify with the death and are troubled with guilt and self-blame;

91

and either because they knew something of the problems of the deceased, or because some of the secrets including the suicidal thoughts of the deceased had been shared with them, or because they had refused to go along with some escapade with the deceased, they now begin to assume responsibility for the death and to feel blamed by the community, including the deceased family. These survivors need time and the opportunity to discuss their feelings openly with a sympathetic adult and the freedom to share their own fears of attempting suicide, before and since their friend's death. Helping the young person break away from any sense of their ownership of the suicide action of their friend is most important and the minister should recognise where some young people might need the help of a professional counsellor in this situation.

Helping each other
De-emphasise suicide – emphasise what people can do to help each other and themselves. The minister very often, in the days immediately following suicide, is in a position to answer truthfully for the close friends and the casual friends of the deceased their questions about the suicide. He is also in a position to discourage the exaggerated rumours that seem inevitably to accompany reports of suicides. But once the facts have been told, it is time to move on from the suicide and to initiate within the community some movement in which the tragedy of suicide can be turned into a learning experience. The pastoral minister can help young people identify trusted and caring adults who are available for counselling or just for a good, long talk. He might consider bringing together a core of agreed volunteers to do this work and having them trained. He, with his team of adults, might also help young people to learn to take care of themselves and to know themselves well enough to get help when they really need it.

Concerns
Deal with their concerns – find out what they are and talk about them. In addressing the suicide which has just been committed, it may be possible for the minister to talk about the combination of stressors that were unique to the individual who committed suicide and to help survivors understand the particular set of circum-

stances that this one young person faced. This can help the survivor identify the particular issues and concerns that bother him or her and then it is possible to move to discussing nondestructive ways of dealing with those problems. This reinforces the idea that other solutions are possible and it addresses the often unspoken thought in the surviving young person, 'maybe suicide is a way out for me too.'

No glory in suicide!
Limit memorialisation – don't glorify the death or prolong the praises and tributes. The minister should be very careful to avoid prolonging attention on the death; by doing this you are decreasing the chance of the 'copycat' effect.

> In planning the funeral with family members, clergy should strive to avoid intensifying the prestige that death may have accorded the young victim. Scheduling a funeral during school hours unfortunately suggests that suicide can stop the young people's world and make everyone take notice ... Glorifying eulogies are a mistake ... small counselling groups can help young people understand that death is permanent and the suicide victim will not gain satisfaction from any post-mortem events. It is important to present suicide as a painfully permanent solution to temporary problems for which help is available.[45]

Extended attention to the death seems to glamorise it in the eyes of the young and feeds the fantasies of other high-risk youth that suicide is a way to get the relief and attention they perceive to be unavailable in any other way. This is difficult for the minister since he does not wish to minimise the loss which parents and family as well as the young people are experiencing. But very often, with the co-operation of the parents and immediate family, many helpful and therapeutic things can be both said and done.

Eliminate access
Eliminate access to the means by which impulsive and depressed youth attempt suicide. It might never be possible to prevent suicide by a truly determined person, but it may be possible to slow

down and deter the impulsive act, the desperate moment, the overwhelmed young person who acts while drinking or in a rage, by making sure that the means of suicide are not readily available. Firearms, drugs and poison are obviously often too readily available and alerting the community to this danger might well be the saving of another young person who feels caught in the self-destructive trap.

Appendices

Funeral Liturgy Arrangements

Name of Deceased

Commonly known as

Address

Date of Death

Funeral Arrangements

Day and Time of Removal

Day and Time and Place of Funeral Mass

Celebrant

With Concelebrants

Burial in

Sacred Music or Hymns Selected :

1.

2.

3.

4.

Readings Selected:
The readings selected should normally be: (a) First Reading taken from the Old Testament, (b) Responsorial Psalm, (c) Second Reading taken from the Epistles, (d) Gospel Reading.

First Reading

to be read by

Responsorial Psalm

to be read (or sung) by

Second Reading _____

to be read by _____

Gospel Acclamation _____

to be read by _____

Gospel _____

to be read by the priest _____

Bidding Prayers:

Intentions: 1. _____

_____ 2. _____

_____ 3. _____

_____ 4. _____

_____ 5. _____

Bidding Prayer Readers:

_____ 1. _____

_____ 2. _____

_____ 3. _____

_____ 4. _____

_____ 5 . _____

Offertory Procession: Gifts:

_____ 1. _____

_____ 2. _____

_____ 3. _____

_____ 4. _____

A survivor's letter

This is a letter composed by Fr Arnaldo Pangrazzi, an American priest who has studied and written widely on the subject of suicide. (I take the text from an article entitled, 'Suicide is not painless' by Fr Brian D'Arcy in *The Sunday World*, December 4th 1988.) The letter is offered as something survivors can sit down and write in their own handwriting to their relative who has committed suicide. I offer it here as a beautiful piece of writing, succinctly bringing together many of the thoughts and feelings of someone who is nearly healed. As an exercise to offer to survivors, I would have some considerable doubts!

My dear ...

As you read this letter, we would like you to know that we miss you and that so much has changed because of you. We always thought that this sort of thing happened to other people, not us. Maybe, in your heart, you thought you were doing us a favour by taking your own life. What hurts most is that you never really said 'goodbye' or gave us a chance to say 'goodbye' to you. We have cried as we tried to change what has been, tried to understand your despair, your misery.

At times we have been angry with you for what you did to yourself, for what you did to us. At times we felt responsible for your death. We have searched for what we did or failed to do, for the clues we missed. Yet we also know that, no matter what, we couldn't choose for you. We are learning to stop feeling responsible for your death. If we were responsible for you, you'd still be alive.

We all think of you so often, even when it hurts to remember. We are really lonely for your presence and whenever we hear your songs, we still cry for you. We feel sad that you're not here to share so many moments with us. That's when our mornings have no beginnings and our nights seem long as winter.

Slowly though, it's getting less hard. We try to remember the good times. Maybe you've seen us smile a little more. We're learning to live again, realising that we cannot die because you chose to die. We pray that you are at peace. At the end of our days, we look forward to being with you again.

Peace.

DOs And DON'Ts

I'm not altogether sure about the usefulness of a 'Do's and Don'ts' list of helpful suggestions, particularly in the case of caring for the grief stricken. However some people thought I should include it as an appendix to have a ready-reckoner for priests with an already over-flowing memory bank! (This list is adapted from a number of sources, but especially the list given at the end of Iris Bolton's book, *'My Son... My Son...'*)

DOs

Do respond honestly to questions asked by the family. You need not answer more than asked. If they want to know more they will ask later. Too much information, too soon can feel hurtful.

Do surround the family with as much love and understanding as you can and ensure that their support is ongoing from within the community.

Do show them love.

Do let them talk. Most of the time they just need to hear out loud what is going on in their heads. Usually they are not wanting advice. Encourage the idea that all decisions are to be made by the family together.

Do allow them to decide for themselves what they are ready for. Offer your ideas but let them decide.

If a child has died, *do* pay special attention to that child's brothers and sisters, if any. Do this at the wake, the funeral and in the coming months.

Do allow each family member to express as much grief as they are feeling and are willing to share.

Do encourage them to talk about the special, endearing qualities of the loved one who has died and to talk of their memories of good times shared with that loved one.

DON'Ts

Don't assume you know best.

Don't tell a griever, 'I know just how you feel.' You don't know! Everyone's grief is unique.

Don't make comparisons, like saying, 'I know how you feel because my ... died' or 'When you look at ... can't you see how lucky you are? It might have been worse'

Don't tell then what to feel! Let them feel what they are feeling when they are feeling it.

Don't ever treat them as if they don't have enough sense to make their own decisions or to understand what they are being told.

Don't preach. If religion is important to them, they will draw strength from it. Don't tell them that what has happened is God's will.

Don't try to water down the Church's teaching to make it more 'acceptable' to the griever.

Don't ply them with your personal pain-killers such as alcohol, pills or personal medication. Leave that to the experts.

No matter who has died, *don't* let that person's name be tabooed. If he or she is never mentioned, it seems as if everyone wants to forget that such a person once existed. Most families need to hear the name of their loved one over and over.

Don't let your own sense of helplessness keep you from reaching out to a bereaved person.

Don't try to find something positive (e.g., a moral lesson, closer family ties, a return to practice of the faith) about a loved one's death.

Don't point out, in the case of a child's death, that they have other children. Children are never interchangeable.

Don't make any comment that might imply negligence on the part of family members, medical teams, police or neighbours. Survivors are often plagued enough by feelings of doubt and guilt without needing any help from others.

Don't be sexist in your approach to grievers; men and women both have their grief, and tears are not the prerogative of women. Allow both men and women to grieve in their own way.

The Samaritans

The beginning
A priest called Chad Varah began the Samaritans. First he offered a special help service for the suicidal, with himself as the expert helper. He found that many people did not want to see him if they had told his receptionists about themselves and their troubles while they waited. He decided that many suicidal people were helped by talking to a sympathetic listener. Only a few needed expert help. He started the first Samaritan branch in London, a move which has led to a large charity with 170 branches in Britain and Ireland.

A 24-hour service
All branches offer the same help. The centre is somewhere easy to reach. Nearly always, it can be visited any time of day or evening or telephoned any time, day or night. There will usually be a room with the emergency telephone, an office, and some rooms where callers can talk to a Samaritan worker in private. All workers are volunteers. They are all ages and sorts who have been carefully trained to be sympathetic listeners. They will do a duty of about 5 hours every week or every fortnight.

Who uses the Samaritans?
All sorts of people use the Samaritans, more and more of them young. People find life difficult for many reasons and call the Samaritans with many different problems. Since it is an emergency service, many people call when things are suddenly too much, particularly if they are feeling so bad that they are thinking about suicide. They ring because they want to tell someone how they feel. Some people want to be advised but find that, when they have talked about it, they know themselves what they want to do. Often they do not have to do anything – they just need someone to listen.

What help do they get?
Callers are befriended. A volunteer acts like a sympathetic friend. Sometimes there will be only one visit or call, other times a caller

may want to keep in contact until things are going better. If decisions have to be taken, the Samaritan volunteer helps the caller think about the different results of different actions. Above all the volunteer tries to make it easy for the caller to talk about how he feels, about why everything is so awful. No information is passed on to anybody; not parents, not friends, not police, not school, unless the caller wants it. A caller does not have to give a name. It is because people know that help is confidential, and they can remain anonymous, that they use the Samaritans.

Are the Samaritans any help?
Because a quarter of a million people use the Samaritans for the first time in a year, it is clear that many people want this sort of help. If the Samaritans were no use, people would stop coming. At the same time, as more and more people used the Samaritans, the suicide rate dropped by a third in England and Wales. This may have been partly because of the Samaritans. No other country has a service like this and no other country has seen such a drop in suicide. Certainly many people who use the Samaritans talk about suicide; many find it a great help to talk to someone who has time to listen. Sadly suicide is now increasing slowly and attempted suicide is increasingly rapidly. But the Samaritans are not concerned only with suicide. People come to talk over all sorts of problems.

Erwin Stengel, a British psychiatrist who made a special study of suicide and attempted suicide, wrote of the Samaritans:

There is no doubt that they do prevent suicides; but it is not possible to estimate how great is their contribution to the decline of the suicide rate or the degree to which they prevent suicidal crises from developing in the future.

Bill Blackburn, *What you should know about Suicide*, Word Publishing Dallas 1990. Contains comprehensive information about the subject of suicide.

Christopher Lukas & Henry M. Seiden, *Silent Grief: Living in The Wake of Suicide*, Papermac, London 1990. They deal very well the the difficulty of coping experienced by familles and in particular the phenomenon of bargaining following a suicide.

Archbishop Dermot Clifford, *Suicide: A permanent solution to a temporary problem?* A Pastoral letter, Veritas Publications, Dublin 1990. A short and very readable pamphlet, sensitive and yet firm on Church teaching.

Iris Bolton (with Curtis Mitchell), *My Son... My Son..., A guide to healing after death, loss or suicide,* Bolton Press, Atlanta, Georgia 1983. A moving story of a mother's road to recovery following the suicide of her son and of her work to help others who find themselves in this difficulty.

Linda Rosenfield and Marilynne Prupas, *Left Alive After a Suicide in the Family,* Charles C. Thomas Publisher, Springfield, Illinois 1984. Some very worthwhile insights but lacks (deliberately avoids) religious insights.

Lois A. Bloom, *Mourning After Suicide,* The Pilgrim Press, New York 1989. A short, readable and very helpful pamphlet and certainly something that could be left with a family after their bereavement.

Therese A. Rando, *Grief, Dying and Death: Clinical Interventions for Caregivers,* Research Press Co., Illinois 1984. Gives tremendous insights into a very wide range of issues concerned with grief, dying and death.

James T. Clemons (ed), *Perspectives on suicide,* Westminster/John Knox Press, Louisville, Kentucky 1990. A series of worthwhile essays on the various perspectives on suicide. In particular, I found the essay on pastoral perspectives and psychological perspectives most helpful.

Earl Grollman, *Suicide: Prevention, Intervention, Postvention*, Beacon Press, Boston 1988. A book from a leading expert, but I found it a little disappointing on the 'postvention' side of suicide.

Donna Reilly Williams & JoAnn Sturzl, *Grief Ministry: Helping others Mourn*, Resource Publications, San Jose, California 1990. A wonderful book on grief ministry with many challenging insights.

James T. Clemons (ed), *Sermons on Suicide*, Westminster/John Knox Press, Louisville, Kentucky 1989. Interesting to see how other pastoral ministers treated of the subject in religious services outside of a Funeral Mass.

1. *Trends in Suicide: N. Ireland 1960-86*, by P.S. Curran, R.J. Finlay and P.J. McGarry, published in *Irish Journal of Psychological Medicine* (1988), 5 pp. 98-102

2. St Augustine, *City of God*, Book One, Chapters 17-27. Extracts from a new translation by Henry Bettenson, Penguin Classics, London 1984.

3. Text taken from *Declaration on Euthanasia*, English translation published in *Vatican II: More Post Conciliar Documents*, ed. Austin Flannery, OP, Dominican Publications, Dublin 1982.

4. Häring, Bernard, *Medical Ethics*, St Paul Publications, Slough England 1972.

5. Peschke, C. Henry, *Christian Ethics, A Presentation of Special Moral Theology in the Light of Vatican II*, Vol II, Goodliffe Neale, Alcester and Dublin 1978.

6. As quoted in 'Can faith survive a suicide in the family?', article in *U. S. Catholic* by Jean Davidson, November 1987.

7. *Suicide, A permanent solution to a temporary problem?* A Pastoral Letter by Dermot Clifford, Archbishop of Cashel and Emly, Veritas Publications, Dublin 1990.

8. *ibid*.

9. Hewett, John H., *After Suicide*, Westminster Press, Philadelphia 1980.

10. Gooden W.E., 'Suicide Research', *Dictionary of Pastoral Care and Counselling*, ed. Hunter, Rodney J., Abingdon Press, Nashville 1990.

11. c.f. Bolton, Iris, *My Son...My Son...*, *A guide to healing after death, loss or suicide*, Bolton Press, Atlanta, 1983, Chapter 8.

12. Shneidman, *Suicide*, p.1774.

13. These are excellently explored in Blackburn, Bill, *What you should know about Suicide*, Word Publishing, Dallas 1990, and his listing is presented here.

14. Robinson, Rita, *Survivors of Suicide*, IBS Press, Santa Monica, 1989, p. 91.

15. Shneidman, Edwin S., 'Foreword' in Albert C. Cain, ed., *Survivors of Suicide*, Charles C Thomas, Springfield, Illinois 1972.

16. Wright,Wasena F. Jr., 'Suicide: An Unpardonable Sin', published in *Sermons on Suicide*, ed., James T. Clemons, Westminster/John Knox Press, Louisville, Kentucky 1989.

17. *Pastoral Care of the Sick, Rites of Anointing and Viaticum*, English translation, Veritas Publications and Geoffrey Chapman, Dublin and London, 1983.

18. *ibid.*

19. *ibid.*

20. Bolton, Iris, *My Son... My Son...*, *A guide to healing after death, loss or suicide*, Bolton Press, Atlanta, 1983, p. 16.

21. *Order of Christian Funerals*, Veritas Publications, Dublin 1991. (Vatican Council II, *Constitution on the Liturgy, Sacrosanctum Concilium*, Art.5).

22. Rando, Therese, *Grief, Dying and Death, Clinical Interventions for Caregivers*, Research Press Co., Illinois 1984.

23. Champlin, Joseph, *Through Death To Life, Preparing to Celebrate the Mass of Christian Burial*, Ave Maria Press, Indiana 1979.

24. *Order of Christian Funerals*, Veritas Publications, Dublin 1991.

25. 'The Funeral Homily: A Theological View', Robert A. Kreig, *Worship*, May 1984, pp. 222-238.

26. Häring, Bernard, *Medical Ethics*, St Paul Publications, Slough England 1972.

27. 'The Funeral Homily: A Theological View', Robert A. Kreig, *Worship*, May 1984, pp. 222-238.

28. *ibid.*

29. 'God's Ultimate Claim', by W. Guy Delaney in *Sermons on Suicide*, ed. James T. Clemons, Westminster/John Knox Press, Kentucky 1989.

30. *Order of Christian Funerals*, Veritas Publications, Dublin 1991.

31. *Order of Christian Funerals*, Veritas Publications, Dublin 1991.

32. I use the word 'suicide' here to demonstrate how it might be used, aware of the points made in an earlier paragraph, *Do we mention suicide?*, quoting Bernard Häring.

33. Parker, Morgan A. Jr., 'Pastoral Care Perspectives', published in *Perspectives on Suicide*, ed. James T. Clemons, Westminster/John Knox Press, Kentucky 1990.

34. Lindemann, Erich, and Greer, Ina May, 'A Study of Grief: Emotional Responses to Suicide', *Pastoral Psychology*, December 1953, p. 9-13.

35. Rosenfield, Linda and Prupas, Marilynne, *Left Alive: After a Suicide Death in the Family*, Charles C. Thomas Publisher, Springfield, Illinois 1984.

36. Bolton, Iris, *My Son... My Son...*, *A guide to healing after death, loss or suicide*, Bolton Press, Atlanta, 1983.

37. Lukas, Christopher and Seiden, Henry M., *Silent Grief, Living in the Wake of Suicide*, Papermac Publishers, London,1990.

38. *ibid.*, pp. 53-54.

39. Lindemann, Erich, 'Symptomatology and Management of Acute Grief', *Journal of Pastoral Care*, V.5 No. 3, 1951, pp. 19-31.

40. This process is explored in Kübler-Ross, Elizabeth, *On Death and Dying*, Tavistock Publications, London 1970.

41. The theories are summarised here using Benson, Jenny, *Bereavement, A Guide for Nurses*, Lippincott Nursing Series, Harper & Row Publishers, London 1990.

42. Benson, Jenny, *Bereavement, A Guide for Nurses*, Lippincott Nursing Series, Harper & Row Publishers, London 1990.

43. Bonnett Stein, Sara, 'About Dying', as quoted in *Helping a Child Grieve and Grow*, Care Notes published by Abbey Press, St Meinrad, Indiana 1990.

44. Bolton, Iris, *My Son... My Son...*, *A guide to healing after death, loss or suicide*, Bolton Press, Atlanta, 1983.

45. Davidson, Lucy, 'Psychological Perspectives', in *Perspectives on Suicide*, ed. James T. Clemons, Westminster/John Knox Press, Kentucky 1990.

2304